We Look Like This

DAN BURT was born in South Philadelphia in 1942. He attended state schools and a local Catholic college before reading English at St John's College, Cambridge. After graduating from Yale Law School he practised law in the United States, Saudi Arabia and Britain before moving to London in 1994 and becoming a British citizen. He is an Honorary Fellow of St John's College and lives and writes in London and Cambridge. His poetry publications include the pamphlets *Searched For Text* (2008) and *Certain Windows* (2011), and *Cold Eye*, a collaboration with the artist Paul Hodgson (2010), all published by Carcanet Press in the Lintott Press imprint. His poetry was included in Carcanet's *New Poetries V* anthology and has been published in periodicals including the *TLS*, *Poetry Review*, *The New Statesman*, *Financial Times* and *PN Review*. Visit www.danburtpoetry.com for further information about Dan Burt's poetry.

Also by Dan Burt from Carcanet Press

Searched For Text
Certain Windows
Cold Eye (with Paul Hodgson)

★

DAN BURT

We Look Like This

CARCANET

First published in Great Britain in 2012 by
Carcanet Press Limited
Alliance House
Cross Street
Manchester M2 7AQ

www.carcanet.co.uk

A CIP catalogue record for this book is available from the British Library

ISBN 978 1 84777 132 2
ISBN 978 1 84777 197 1 (with Lintott Press)

The publisher acknowledges financial assistance from Arts Council England

Typeset by XL Publishing Services, Tiverton
Printed and bound in England by SRP Ltd, Exeter

for J.R. and A.C.

Acknowledgements

Some of the poems in this book were previously published in *The Eagle*, *The Courtauld News*, *Financial Times*, *The Grove*, *The New Statesman*, *Newsletter of the Institute for Advanced Study*, *PN Review*, *Poetry Review*, *TLS* and *New Poetries V* (Carcanet, 2011).

A Note on the Text

The poems in this book use a mixture of British and American English, while the prose memoir uses wholly American English. This is not inadvertence, but a deliberate decision on the author's part.

Contents

I

Who He Was

(Joe Burt 1915–1995)

1

He catapulted from his armchair,
airborne for an instant, primed to smash
the fledgling power who dared challenge
his rule. That runty five-year-old who would
not stop his catch to fetch a pack of Luckys
crossed some unmarked border, threatened
the kingdom's order and loosed the dogs of war.

No chance to repent, no strap, no bruises
on my face, my mother's screaming just static
behind the pounding taking place; rage spent,
sortie ended, he thumped down the stairs
to his crushed velvet base, pending new
provocations to launch him into space.

Worse followed till my biceps hardened,
but that first strike left most scars: with strangers
six decades on klaxons *ahwooga*,
the clogged heart hammers, I weigh my chance.

2

A scion of the tents of Abraham
born during World War I, he policed
a patriarch's long list of rights: no one
but he sat in the fat feather armchair
confronting the TV, or at our table's
head, read the paper before he did or
said *Let's go somewhere else* when we ate out;
if he fell sick the house fell silent, roared
and we all quaked.

I was chattel as well
as son and he sold my youth for luxuries:
an extra day a week to fish, lunch time
shags with his cashier, a kapo's trades.

My anger, like an old Marxist's, leached
away as parenthood, mistakes and time
taught Moloch is a constant. Attic myth,
Old Testament, bulge with sacrificial
tales, the Crucifixion one more offering
to Baal; families recapitulate
phylogeny, it's what fathers do.

3

the golden land in the 'thirties

Morning he threads russet gorges
of two-story brick row houses –
short pants, pals, eighth grade
shut behind him – and evening
draggles home past trolleys full
of profiles who paid the nickel
he can't afford to ride.
                  No one
waits dinner: his mother leaves cold
soup in the kitchen (on Fridays
chicken) he gobbles by the sink
and chases with a fag puffed
on the way to box, while siblings,
older, younger, scribble lessons
or meet friends; sleeps alone
above the back porch in an unheated
room; wears his brother's hand-me-
downs; his father beats him bloody
for spending part of his first pay-
check on a first pair of new shoes;

for cash he boxes bantam weight
before crowds shrieking *kill the kike,*

hawks sandwiches from wooden carts
to high school kids who once were friends,
at quitting time shoots crap with men
and at sixteen, meat hook in hand,
stands in a butcher shop's ice-box
breaking beef hindquarters down.

Depression shadowing the Volk
like a Canaanite colossus,
arms bent at elbows, palms turned up,
hefts the male offering, sublimes
skin so it no longer feels pain,
fuses eyelids so rainbows shine
in vain, sears nerves so hands cannot
unclench and a decade on, when
ritual ends, amid ashes
the sacrifice survives, savage
more than man, hard, violent,
unbelieving, in the orbit
of whose fists lie his certainties.

4

Bouts sometimes knocked him head to knees,
His swollen gut spewed crimson
Shit, he wasted until Crohn's disease
Left his great white hope the surgeon.

Tangled in tubes and drips post-op,
Missing most of his ileum,
Ribs prominent through cotton top,
Fed strained juice and pabulum
He went fifteen rounds with death.

The dark heavyweight danced away,
Doctors raised his withered arm
And sent him south where snowbirds play
Hoping he'd recover weight and form.

There he eyed the champion
Crouched outside the ring to spring
Back for the rematch no one wins,
His belly's serpentine stitching,
The black before, the black after.

And when again he spread the ropes
Apart, he could not see beyond
Himself and his ringside shadow.

5

The skeleton in a wheelchair props rented
tackle on the rail, stares down twenty feet
from a pier through salt subtropical air
at shoal water wavelets for blue slashes
flashing toward the bait below his float,
and misses one hit, two, a third, an inept
young butcher far from inner-city streets
recovering from surgery, too proud
to bask with codgers, too weak to walk or swim,
a sutured rag doll whose one permitted
sport is dangling blood worms from a pole.

His father's plumb and adze, mother's thread and pins,
tradesmen, carters, peddlers, kaftaned bearded
kin, village landsmen from Ukraine, friends, nothing
in his life smelled of ocean; but cleaver
held again, he kept on fishing. Once a week
he drove eighty miles east to prowl the sea
with charter-men, ever farther from the coast
till, white coat and meat hook junked, he trolled
ballyhoo for marlin eight hours' run offshore.

Two score and four skiffs on, by his command
we laid him down in fishing clothes, khaki
trousers, khaki shirt, *Dan-Rick* on the right
breast pocket, on the left *Capt. J. Burt*.

Death Mask

(L.K.B. 1917–2008)

I would have cast a death mask from her head
Cooling in a bed ringed by surviving kin
If plaster of Paris drying on shrunken
Skin, dull black buttons that had been eyes
And bared grey gums could model havoc
Ninety years had wrought upon a beauty.
But how we ruin others leaves no mark
To be traced: fixing her husband's family
Dinner bequeathed no scars to Procne's face.

I took a twelve-inch square of putty-coloured
Construction paper, drew a pear, inverted,
Eight inches long, four wide for cheeks to flare,
Made marks for spud nose, a Bacon mouth,
Wisps of white hair, spite lines, spots,
Scissored the outline, scraped fascia from frame
Like spittle from sere lips: but I'm no artist
With stroke and scumble to express the natural
History of families in a screaming rictus.

I turned the womb shape over and wrote how
My heels rucked the kitchen rug as she dragged
Me out at five to fight a bully, and watched;
How smart she looked, fresh from the hairdresser,
Made up and gloved to shop, after she dropped
Her eighth-grade butcher boy at his weekend work;
How if lover lift a hand to caress my cheek
I flinch. Dear Spartan mother, why did you send me
To the Apothetae, alone among your children?

I sat staring in my study at the ju-ju I'd made
Then from a top shelf pulled a thick book down
From psychologies I now won't read again,
Opened it in the middle, laid the damned thing
Between the pages as you would to press a flower,
Or billets-doux from a bad affair you can't quite
Forget, and committed her to my high loculus.

15

Slowly Sounds the Bell

Nunc lento sonitu dicunt, morieris.
Now this bell tolling softly for another,
says to me, Thou must die.

Donne, Meditation XVII

A midnight ring from half a world away
Tolls my only brother's sudden death.
Line dead, handset re-cradled, sleep returns;
I wake to find bedclothes scarcely messed.

We long were distant islands to each other –
I stood Esau to his Jacob as a boy,
My fields the sea, his tents the libraries –
DNA proved inadhesive, no gene
Sutured the rifts between us, and the news
Was less vexing than a tree fall in my garden.

We hope for more: a foetal element
Feeding fondness for our kin, a shared
Enzyme sealing first cousins best of friends,
From propinquity Gileadan balm.

But boyhood hatred, dumb decades apart,
Change blood to water, degauss genealogies;
Abel becomes Cain's pathogen. A shrug
In the cell metastasises through
Isolate null points of the tribe into
Skull paddies and black snow in June.

Religious tapestries woven from old deities
Cannot conceal trenches we dig between us:
Ancestral chemistry stands hooded on
The scaffold, testing trap and rope for all.

It is the face on the school run who mouths
'Hello', a torso hunched on the next bar stool
Twice a week, a high school sweetheart back,
A man selling ceramics I collect
Dying of AIDS, whose curfews heave the clapper
Summoning tears, the shiver in the neck.

II

Certain Windows

We trail no clouds of glory when we come. We trail blood, a cord that must be cut and post-partum mess that mix with places, people, and stories to frame the house of childhood. We dwell in that house forever.

In time there will be others, bigger, smaller, better, worse; but how we see the world, how much shelter, warmth, food we think we need, whether the outer dark appears benign or deadly depend on what we saw from certain windows in that house. We may burn, rebuild, repaint or raze it, but its memories fade the least; as dementia settles in the first things are the last to go.

Despite the enduring brightness of childhood's colors we may touch them up, sometimes garishly, to infuse the humdrum with romance as we grow old. Testosterone wanes, breasts sag, but in some, perhaps secretly in most, the adolescent hunger to allure and seduce, swagger and swash-buckle remains.

The inherent dishonesty and danger of romantic reconstruction are reasons enough to try to record as accurately as possible what we saw, if we record at all. Vanity's subversions are another; respect for acquaintances, editor and the few readers interested in context or what appears unusual a third. Last, there is the flicker rekindling the past throws on why someone picks up pen, or brush or camera.

Childhood ended when I turned twelve and began working in a butcher shop on Fridays after school and all day Saturdays from 7 a.m. to 6 p.m., or, as we said in winter, "from can't see to can't see." By sixteen I was working thirty hours a week or more during the school year, and fifty to sixty hours in the summers. This is a recollection of my pre-travailous world, of places, people and tales from childhood.

1. Ancestral Houses

Fourth and Daly

Joe Burt, my father, was born in Boston in 1916, almost nine months to the day after his mother landed there from a *shtetl* near Kiev. She brought with her Eva, her first-born, and Bernie, her second. Presumably my grandfather Louis, Zaida ("*ai*" as in *pay*) or Pop, was pleased to see my grandmother, Rose, or Mom, even though she was generally regarded as a *chaleria*, Yiddish for "shrew."

Zaida had been dragooned into the Russian army a little before World War I broke out. Russia levied a quota of Jewish men for the army from each *shtetl* and these men invariably came from the poorest *shtetlachim*. Zaida deserted at the earliest opportunity, which was certainly not unusual, made his way to Boston and sent for Mom.

Mom and Pop moved the family in 1917 to a small row (terraced) house at Fourth and Daly streets in South Philadelphia, the city where my father grew up, worked, married and in 1995 died. Pop was a carpenter, Mom a seamstress, both socialists at least, if not Communists. Mom was an organizer for the I.L.G.W.U. (the International Ladies' Garment Workers' Union), which seems in character. Yiddish was the household tongue, my father's first, though Pop spoke and read Russian and English fluently. Mom managed Russian well, but English took more effort.

The family's daily newspaper was *Forverts* (*The Forward*), printed in Yiddish. *Forverts* published lists of those killed in pogroms when they occurred. Ukrainian Cossacks allied themselves with the Bolsheviks and used the Russian civil war as an excuse to continue the pogroms that had been a fact of Jewish life in the Pale from the 1880s. Pop was hanging from a trolley car strap on his way home from work in 1920 when he read the names of his family among the dead, all eighteen of them: father, mother, sisters, brothers, their children. He had become an orphan. He never went to *schul* (synagogue) again.

A few years later he learned how they were killed when some of Mom's family, who had hidden during the raid, emigrated to America. I heard the story from him when I was ten, at Christmas 1952. I came home singing "Silent Night," just learned in my local public elementary school. I couldn't stop singing it and went caroling up the back steps from the alley into our kitchen where Pop, putty-colored, in his mid-sixties and dying of cancer, was making what turned out to be his last visit. Zaida had cause to dislike Gentile sacred songs, though I didn't know it. He croaked *Danila, shah stil* (*Danny, shut up*) and I answered *No, why should I?* His face flushed with all the life left in him and he grabbed me by the neck and began to choke me. My father pulled him off, pinioned his arms, and, when his rage passed, led me to the kitchen table where Zaida sat at the head and told me this story:

The Jews had warning of a raid. Pop's father, my great-grandfather, was pious and reputed to be a *melamed*, a learned though poor Orthodox Jew. As such he was prized and protected by the community. Pop's in-laws urged him to take his family and hide with them in their shelter below the street. Great-grandfather refused. He said, I was told, *God will protect us*.

The Cossacks rousted them from their house and forced everyone to strip. They raped the women while the men watched. Done, they shot them, then the children and, last, the men. They murdered all eighteen, my every paternal forebear except Pop, who died an atheist, as did my father.

My grandparents' house at Fourth and Daly was a three-up, three-down row home on a very narrow street. People parked their cars on the side of the street opposite their house, leaving just room enough for a small car to pass; big-finned 'fifties Caddys, had anyone owned one, would have had to straddle the pavement to negotiate their street. The front door stood two feet from the sidewalk at the top of three marble steps with dips in their middle from eighty years of footsteps and repeated scrubbings. It opened into a tiny vestibule off a living room, after which came dining room and kitchen, all three no more than twelve by fourteen. There was a four-foot-wide wooden stoop past the back door two steps above a small concrete yard where clothes hung to dry and children could play. A six-foot-high wooden fence enclosed the yard.

Nothing hung on the walls: there were no bookcases, books, or Victrola. But there was a large console three-band radio which could receive short-wave broadcasts from Europe. The house was always spotless, sparsely furnished and lifeless. Two low rectangles projected from either party wall to separate the living from dining rooms; on each end of these little walls stood two decorative white wooden Doric columns pretending to hold the ceiling up and give a touch of class to what was in fact a clean brick shotgun shack.

We did not visit Fourth and Daly frequently. My mother was never keen to go, perhaps because she learned too little Yiddish after she married my father to make conversation easily, perhaps because Mom had refused to speak to her until after I was born. (My maternal grandmother had been Italian and hence my mother was a Gentile according to Jewish law.) But while Zaida lived we always went for Seder dinner on the first night of Pesach or Passover, the Jewish holiday commemorating the Exodus from Egypt. That tale had some heft when I first heard it a few years after the fall of Nazi Germany.

My brother and I, six and eight, were dropped off at their house early on the Passover a year or two before Zaida died to watch him and Mom prepare the Passover meal. Boredom soon set in, and Zaida took us out to the back stoop where he produced two blocks of grainy pine and proceeded to carve two *dreidels*, the four-sided top Jewish children have played with for generations. He inscribed letters in Hebrew, the traditional *aleph, beth, gimel, nun*, one on each *dreidel* side, with a hard lead pencil and explained that each letter had a value, from zero to three: the side facing up when it landed after we spun it represented how many nuts, pennies, etc. the other players had to pay the spinner. Then he counted twenty hazelnuts apiece into our hands and set us gambling on the stoop while he went inside to help Mom.

Three things always happened at the Passover dinner. Someone spilled the wine on Mom's white lace tablecloth, producing a scramble for cold water and lemon juice to wipe it away; there was a fight during which Zaida had to restrain my father; and Zaida lingered over the third son's role in answering the Four Questions (*der fier kashes*). The Four Questions are the heart and *raison d'être* for the Seder, a religious service-cum-dinner to celebrate and teach the story of the Jews' deliverance from Egypt. Shortly after the service begins the youngest boy must ask, *Why is this night different from all others?*, and the leader of the Seder will retell the story of the Exodus, the repeated experience of our wandering tribe's history.

Though Zaida wasn't a believer he was an ethnic realist who wanted his grandchildren to understand that Jewish blood is a perfume that attracts murderers, a pheromone no soap can wash away. So he dwelt on the role of the third son, the wicked one, who asks, *What does this service mean to you?*, implying that he is different, he can be what he wants, that the Seder and his blood's history mean nothing to him. The answer ordained for this son is, *It is because of what the Lord did for me*, not you, i.e. had you been there you'd have been left to die.

Today the *dreidel* Zaida made me lies on my desk in London, as it has lain on other desks in other cities, other countries down the years. I don't know what happened to the one he made for my brother, who was cremated, a Christian, in San Francisco in 2005.

At Fourth and Daly my father, Joe everywhere else, was always *Yossela*, Joey. He was a thin, short man, five feet five, with intense blue eyes, dark skin and thick black hair. He could easily have passed for an Argentinian tangoist, or a Mafia hit-man; perhaps the latter image had attracted my mother to him. Broad thick shoulders, large hands and well-muscled legs perfectly suited the featherweight semi-pro boxer he had become.

Lust and rage beset his every age. His fists rose at the slightest provocation against all comers and sometimes against me. Bullies and every form of authority were his favored targets. When he was ten a local teenager who had been tormenting him was struck from behind with a lead pipe one winter night. When he came to in hospital several hours and sixteen stitches later, he could recall only that he was passing the Borts' house when something hit him. He gave little Joey no more trouble.

From time to time after I was nine he would take me to help in his butcher shop on Sundays, washing platters, cleaning cases, sweeping the floor and sprinkling fresh sawdust. We drove there in an old Phillip Morris delivery truck, a brown van with only a driver's seat. I sat on a spare tire where the passenger's seat should have been and held on to the door. One Sunday driving home from the store, Joe saw two bigger boys beating a smaller one beside the S.K.F. ball-bearing factory. He hit the brakes, leapt out and knocked down both older boys, then waited till the victim escaped. He hated bullies.

The Depression scarred him. He was twelve when it began. There was little work for carpenters, and for a time Yossela stood on a street corner hawking apples with Zaida. But the family needed more money, so at thirteen he left school without completing the eighth grade and found work in a butcher shop on Fourth Street, a mile or so north of Fourth and Daly. His older sister and both brothers, older and younger, all finished high school. My father regretted his lack of formal education and suffered the untutored's awe of the educated all his life.

Yossela spent part of his first pay check on a new pair of shoes. Zaida beat him when he turned over that first week's earnings minus the cost of the shoes. The legend was that his father's belt struck him so hard there were bloodstains from his ass on the ceiling.

Jewish boys undergo two rituals: circumcision at birth, about which they presumably remember nothing, and, at thirteen, Bar Mitzvah, when they are called on a Saturday morning to read a passage from the Torah before the congregation as part of a rite admitting them to Jewish manhood. A celebration follows, however small, for family and friends. My father left the synagogue immediately after his Bar Mitzvah, changed his clothes and went straight to work, Saturday being the busiest business day of the retail week.

Ninth and Race

Prostitution, gambling, fencing, contract murder, loan sharking, political corruption and crime of every sort were the daily trade in Philadelphia's Tenderloin, the oldest part of town. The Kevitch family ruled this stew for half a century, from Prohibition to the rise of Atlantic City. My mother was a Kevitch.

Not all Jewish boys become doctors, lawyers, violinists or Nobelists: some sons of immigrants from the Pale became criminals, often as part of or in cahoots with Italian crime families. A recent history calls them "tough Jews:" men like Meyer Lansky and Bugsy Siegel, who organized and ran Murder Incorporated for Lucky Luciano in the twenties and thirties; and Arnold Rothstein, the model for Meyer Wolfsheim in *The Great Gatsby*, who fixed the 1919 baseball World Series.[*] The Kevitch family were tough Jews.

Their headquarters during the day was Milt's Bar and Grill at Ninth and Race, the heart of the Tenderloin and two miles north of Fourth and Daly. At night one or more male clan members supervised the family's "after-hours Club" a few blocks away. We called Milt's Bar "the Taproom" and the after-hours club "the Club."

The Taproom stood alone between two vacant lots carpeted with broken bricks and brown beer bottle shards. Bums, beggars, prostitutes and stray cats and dogs littered the streets around it; the smell of cat and human piss was always detectable, mixed with smoke from cigarette and cigar butts smoldering on the pavement where they had been tossed. Milt's was a rectangular two-story building sixty feet long and eighteen wide. It fronted on the cobbles of Ninth Street and through the back door onto a cobbled alley. Both front and back doors were steel; the back door was never locked. The front window was glass block set in the Taproom's brown brick façade like a glass eye in an old soldier's face. It could stop a fairly large-caliber bullet and the wan light filtering through it brightened only the first few feet of the bar, the rest of which was too dark to make out faces.

[*] Rick Cohen, *Tough Jews*, Simon & Schuster, 1998.

More warehouse than pub, the Taproom served no food and little liquor. It was dank and smelled of stale beer, with too few customers to dispel either. I never saw more than a rummy or two drinking, or in the evenings perhaps a few sailors and a whore. The bar ran from the front door for a school bus length towards the rear, with maybe twelve stools in front of it. Three plain iron tables stood near the back door with two iron chairs each. One of these tables stood beside a large colorful Wurlitzer jukebox that played only when a Kevitch – Abe, Big Milt, Meyer or Albert – sat there to talk with someone. On those occasions one had to wonder how the two men heard each other and why their table was placed so close to the Wurlitzer it drowned them out.

I never visited the Club, which began life as a "speakeasy" during Prohibition. My mother's father, Milton or Big Milt (to distinguish him from his nephew Little Milt), and his brother Abe owned the Club and a nearby illegal still. "G-men," i.e. federal Treasury agents, raided the still one day, razed it and dumped its barrels of illegal alcohol in the gutters of the Tenderloin. Abe and Big Milt stood in the crowd as their hootch went down the drain and cheered the G-men on, as upright citizens should. The Kevitch family owned the Club for years after Big Milt and Abe died.

Big Milt was a Republican state legislator elected consistently for decades to represent the Tenderloin ward, which continued to vote ninety percent Republican for many years after the rest of the city went Democratic. It moved into the Democratic camp by a similar ninety per cent margin after the Kevitch family struck a deal with the Democratic leadership in the early fifties. I had little contact with Big Milt. He was a distant figure who drove a luxury car, a big black Lincoln Continental his state salary could not have paid for. He did not like my name and preferred to call me Donald. One birthday present from him of a child's camp chair had "Donald" stenciled across its canvas back. He handled what might politely be called governmental relations for the family, and died in the Club one night, aged sixty-seven, of a massive lung hemorrhage brought on by tuberculosis.

His brother Abe headed the Kevitch family and ran the "corporation," the family loan-sharking business, along with the numbers bank,* gambling, fencing, prostitution and protection.

* "Numbers rackets" or "numbers games" were illegal lotteries, played in poor urban neighborhoods and run, at high profits, by local racketeers.

27

When I got into trouble with the police as a teenager, Uncle Abe told me what to say to the judge at my hearing and what the judge would do, then sat in the back of the courtroom as the judge gave me a second chance and I walked without a record. Abe sat on a folding canvas chair in front of the Taproom in good weather with a cigar in his mouth. Men came up to him from time to time to talk, and sometimes they would go inside to the table beside the jukebox and talk while the music played. Inclement days and winters found him behind the bar. All serious family matters were referred to Abe until he retired and Meyer, the elder of his two sons, took over.

Meyer always greeted me with *Hello shit ass* when my mother took us to the Taproom for a visit. He sat on the same chair outside the bar in good weather as had his father, and had the same conversations beside the jukebox. But unlike Abe he did not live in the Tenderloin, his Italian wife wore minks and diamonds, and his son attended college before becoming a meat jobber with lucrative routes that dwindled after his father died. Also unlike Abe, Meyer traveled, to Cuba before Castro, Las Vegas and, in the 'seventies, Atlantic City.

My father, Joe, began playing in a local poker game and on his first two visits won rather a lot of money. The men running the game knew he was married to Meyer's cousin. They complained to Meyer that they could not continue to let Joe win and Meyer told my father not to play there again because the game was fixed. Joe ignored him. At his next session they cleaned him out.

Meyer had a surprising reach. Joe briefly owned a meat business with a partner, Marty, that did well for eighteen months, after which the partners quarreled bitterly and Joe bought Marty out. A year later agents from the criminal division of the Internal Revenue Service (I.R.S.) began investigating my father's affairs to discover whether he had been evading taxes by not reporting cash sales, which he and many other owners of cash businesses in the fifties most certainly had done. The agents were getting closer and jail loomed.

Joe spoke to Meyer, who told him several days later, *Joe, it'll cost $10,000*, a large sum then and one Joe couldn't raise. Meyer suggested he ask his ex-partner to pay half since the I.R.S. audit covered partnership years. Marty told my father, *I'll give it to you when you need it for bread for your kids*. Joe told Meyer what had happened, but the price remained $10,000. Joe put a second mortgage on our house, which Abe co-signed, paid Meyer, and three days later the I.R.S. agent called and said *Mr. Burt, I don't know who you know, and I don't know how you did it, but I've had a call from the I.R.S. National Office in Washington D.C. ordering me to close this case in one week.*

A year later the I.R.S. criminal investigators returned, this time to audit Marty. Nothing Marty's tax lawyers could do put them off. He begged Joe to ask Meyer for help. But this time Meyer claimed there was nothing he could do. Marty endured a very long trial which ended in a hung jury. Before the I.R.S. could retry him he dropped dead of a heart attack; he was forty-six.

My mother's brother Albert was a taciturn man. He lived with his wife, Babe, née Marian D'Orazio, and their four girls in a row home at Twenty-fourth and Snyder in South Philadelphia's Italian neighborhood. He had no son. Babe was a great beauty, hence the nickname which she still bears proudly at ninety-two, and her daughters were beautiful as well. From the street their house looked like any other working-class row home in the neighborhood, but inside it brimmed with toys, televisions, clothes and delicacies. The daughters were pampered and much envied. Education for Uncle Al, Aunt Babe and their daughters stopped with South Philly High. They attended neither church nor synagogue. There were no books on their tables nor art on their walls, excepting a mural of a bucolic Chinese landscape painted on their living room wall.

Uncle Al was a detective on the Vice Squad, the Philadelphia Police Department's special unit charged with reducing prostitution, gambling, loan sharking, fencing, protection and other rackets. The opportunities for corruption were many; some said the Vice Squad's function was to protect vice. Clarence Ferguson was the head of the Vice Squad. Babe's sister was Ferguson's wife.

We went to visit Uncle Al's house one Sunday when I was ten. A week before, Billy Meade, the boss of the Republican machine in Philadelphia, had been shot and nearly killed in the Club. He was drinking in the early hours at his accustomed spot at the bar when someone shot him with a silenced pistol shoved through the inspection grille in the door when its cover was slid aside in answer to a knock. The shooter apparently was short, because he stood on a milk crate to fire through the grille, must have known Meade could be found in the Club in the wee hours of Sunday morning, and where along the bar he customarily stood.

Billy Meade and Big Milt, Uncle Al's father, were on the outs at the time and Meade had done something that caused Big Milt real trouble. Uncle Al was just five feet five, had ample experience with and access to firearms, and would have known Meade frequented the Club. I watched the police take Uncle Al from his house that morning and confiscate a large chest containing his sword and gun collection. He was tried but not convicted because the murder weapon was never found, and Babe said he had been making love to her in their marriage bed when the shooting occurred. No one else was accused of the attempted murder, and when Meade recovered he made peace with Big Milt. They both died of natural causes.

Some years later Uncle Al was again involved in a shooting, and this time there was no question that he was the shooter. He had stopped for a traffic light in a very rough neighborhood on the way home from work when four young black men approached his car. According to Al they intended to car-jack him. I never saw Uncle Al without his gun, a .38 police revolver he wore in a holster on his belt. When he drove he always unholstered the gun and laid it on the seat beside him. One of the men tried to open the driver's door and Uncle Al grabbed his gun from the seat and shot through the window, seriously wounding him. The other three fled and Al chased them, firing as he went. He brought down a second and the other two were picked up by the police a short time later.

The papers were full of pictures of the car's shattered windows, the two black casualties and the white off-duty detective who had shot them. The police department commended him for bravery. I never saw Uncle Al rage; crossed, he would stare at you coolly with diamond blue eyes and, sooner or later, inevitably, even the score and more.

All the Kevitch men of my grandparents' and my parents' generation had mistresses and did not disguise the fact. Their wives and all the mistresses were Gentiles, excepting Abe's wife, Annie. Uncle Al had a passion for Italian women and consorted openly with his Italian mistress for the last twenty-five years of his life. Divorce was not unheard of in the family, but Al died married to Babe.

One of Uncle Al's daughters described her father by saying, *He collected*. The things he collected included antique swords, guns, watches and jewelry, as well as delinquent principal and interest on extortionate loans the family "corporation" made; protection money from shopkeepers, pimps, madams, numbers writers, gambling dens, thieves and racketeers; and gifts from the Philadelphia branch of the Gambino Mafia family run by Angelo "the gentle don" Bruno. Joe and Uncle Al died within months of each other, and at Joe's funeral Babe proudly told me how Al would make the more difficult collections, say from a gambler who refused to pay his debts. He would cradle his .38 in the flat of his hand and curl his thumb through the trigger guard to hold it in place, like a leather palm sewn to a wool glove. Then he'd slap the delinquent hard in the head with this blue steel palm. His collection record was quite good.

Angelo Bruno and Uncle Al were close for years, until Bruno was killed in 1980 at the age of sixty-nine by a shotgun blast to the back of his head. Albert had protected him and his lieutenants from arrest. In exchange Bruno contributed to Uncle Al's collections. Uncle Al often told his daughters what a wonderful, decent, kind man Bruno was and that he did not allow his family to deal in drugs. The Albert Kevitch family held the Don in high regard.

Babe adored her husband and my four cousins adored their father. They were grateful for the luxurious lives he gave them and were proud of the fear he inspired. No one bullied them. Babe called the four girls together before they went to school the day the newspapers broke the story of Al's arrest on suspicion of shooting Billy Meade and told them if anyone asked whether the Al Kevitch suspected of the shooting was their father they should hold their heads up and answer clearly, *Yes*.

My mother, Louise Kevitch, Albert's younger sister, was born to Milton and Anita Kevitch, née Anita Maria Pellegrino, a block or two from the Taproom in 1917. Nine months later my maternal grandmother, Anita, a Catholic, died in the 1918 flu epidemic and her children, Louise and Albert, were taken in by their Italian immigrant grandmother who lived nearby. She raised Louise from the age of two until thirteen in an apartment over her candy store, its profits more from writing numbers than selling sweets. Louise was thirteen when her grandmother died; she lived with Uncle Abe and Aunt Annie in their large house across the street from the Taproom from then until at twenty-five she married my father.

Louise graduated from William Penn High School in central Philadelphia, wore white gloves out and about and shopping in the downtown department stores, went to the beauty parlor once a week and had a "girl," i.e. a black maid, three days a week to clean and iron, though that was a luxury Joe could ill afford. She did not help him in the store. She spoke reverentially of her brother, Al, and his role as a detective on the Vice Squad; of Big Milt, who worked in Harrisburg, and of Uncle Abe and the family "corporation," which would help us should we need it. Meyer was Lancelot to her, though we never quite knew why. Louise constantly invoked the principle of "family" as a mystic bond to honor with frequent visits to Taproom and Kevitches. Joe did all he could to keep us from their ambit. It was a child-rearing battle he won, but not decisively: Louise kept trying to force us closer to her family; husband and wife fought about it for fifty-five years.

My mother never *bensch licht* (lit Friday night candles) or went to *schul*, except on Rosh Hashanah and Yom Kippur (the High Holy Days). She never told us her mother and grandmother were Italian. When Babe revealed the secret to me, Louise didn't speak to her for months. We never knew her father had married another Gentile shortly after her mother, Anita, died and sired aunts and uncles we never met. She never mentioned Big Milt's mistress, Catherine, who was with him at his death. She never explained how four families – Abe and Annie, Meyer's, his brother Milton's first and second ones – lived well on the earnings of what appeared to be a failing bar and after-hours club in the red light district. Why her brother was so important if he was only a detective, how his family lived so well on a detective's salary were never explained. She did not tell us her mink coat was a gift from her brother, or how he came to have it. Any questions about what Uncle Al or Meyer actually did, any suggestion that any Kevitch male was less than a gentleman infuriated her, brought slaps or punishment, and went unanswered. Through her eyes we saw no Angelo Brunos or Billy Meades. We learned about the Kevitches from observation, from what they told us, and from the papers.

2. Childhood's Houses

716 South Fourth
My parents' marriage was a bare-knuckle fight to the death. The early rounds were fought at 716 South Fourth Street, roughly equidistant from Fourth and Daly and Ninth and Race, where I was born in 1942 and lived till I was nearly five. I watched the next

fifteen rounds from a seat at 5141 Whitaker Avenue in the Feltonville section of North Philadelphia where we moved in 1947. The match continued after I left.

Joe and Louise were introduced through mutual friends at a "clubhouse" in South Philadelphia that he and his bachelor friends rented to drink, throw parties and "make out" with their girl friends. Respectable lower-middle-class girls in the late thirties did not allow themselves to be "picked up," nor did they fornicate till married and then perhaps not often. Louise and her girlfriends lived in the Tenderloin, which made their virtue suspect even as it conferred allure. But there was no question Louise Kevitch, Al's sister and Big Milt's daughter, took her maidenhead intact to the wedding sheets: a gynecologist had to remove it surgically after my parents tried and failed for several days to consummate their marriage. This difficulty was a harbinger of my mother's enduring distaste for sex.

She was a quite attractive woman at twenty when they met and shortly after married: five foot, a hundred pounds, brown eyes, slim with good breasts and fine legs, long soft brown hair and the hauteur of someone with roots to hide who sniffed at anything or anyone not quite *comme il faut*. But Louise was unacceptable to grandmother Rose Bort because she was not Jewish, if not for other reasons. Jews trace kinship matrilineally: if your mother is not Jewish then neither are you. Louise would not consider converting. Rose did not attend their wedding.

The waves of Ashkenazim from the Pale who came to Philadelphia from the 1880s through the early 1920s settled near Fourth Street in South Philadelphia. Louise, or Lou as my father called her, went to live with her husband above Joe's Meat Market, the "store," at 716 South Fourth Street in the heart of the cobbled South Fourth Street shopping area. Their home was the top two floors of a three-story, forty-five-by-fourteen-foot brown brick late Victorian building with a coal furnace. The first floor was the Store. A refrigerated meat case ran some twenty feet from the front display window, also refrigerated, to a small area holding basic dry goods, black-eyed peas, lima beans, rice, Bond bread, Carnation canned milk, Campbell soups, tea, Maxwell House ground coffee in airtight tin cans and sugar. The next fifteen feet contained a small cutting room, the "back room," with two butcher blocks, hot and cold water taps and a fifty-gallon galvanized iron drum for washing platters. Behind the cutting room was a ten-by-twelve-foot walk-in ice box where rump and rounds of beef, pork loins, frying chickens and smoked meats waited to be cut up and put on sale in the window or the case. A decoratively stamped tin ceiling ran from the front door to the ice box. I was born two floors above Joe's Meat Market.

The store's front door was almost entirely plate glass so that customers could see we were open if the door was closed; but to avoid missing a sale it almost never was. A screen door was hung in summers to keep out flies. Two-thirds of the way down the store, adjacent to the wall opposite the meat case, was a trapdoor that opened on rickety steps down to the coal bin and furnace in the cellar. The cellar also held fifty-pound sacks of rice, cartons of sugar, other goods, and the rats and roaches that fed on them. You had to tend the furnace once in the middle of the night or the fire would go out, and, once out, it was hard to rekindle.

Behind the case ran the counter, on which meat was wrapped, chopped, cut, or piled while serving a customer. Bags in sizes that held from two to twenty-five pounds were stacked beneath the counter in vertical piles divided by wooden dowels. Mid-way down the counter was the register, which only my father was allowed to open. On a nail under the register hung a loaded .38-caliber revolver and a blackjack (cosh) on a leather strap; a baseball bat leaned against the back wall by the cosh. All three were used at one time or another.

Three scales trisected the top of the refrigerated case. One-pound cardboard boxes of lard for sale were stacked two feet high either side of the scales' weighing pans, making it impossible to see the meat weighed on them. The butcher slid a box of lard onto the scale as he placed the meat on it and then stood back in a *Look Ma, no hands* pose so the customer could see him. Slabs of fatback, salt pork, and bacon also stood in piles on enameled platters atop the case. Beads of grease dripped from these piles onto the platters towards the end of the day in summer. Flies were everywhere, more in summer than winter, but always there.

Out the door next left was a poulterer's where live chickens, ducks and turkeys in cages squawked, honked and gobbled incessantly; the stink of rotten eggs and ammonia from fowl shit mixed with sawdust drifted to the street. These birds were not happy awaiting death and let every passerby know it. To the right was a yarn shop and, next to it, on the corner, the fish store. The odor of rotting fish heads, tails, scales and blood rose from a garbage can beneath the filleting block, stronger on busier days than slow. Carp milled in galvanized tubs, finning and thrashing until Mr. Segal, the fishmonger, thrust his hand among them and snatched the one the customer pointed to. A brief commotion as he yanked it from the tub, then, with his left arm, he held it still on the chopping block while his right severed head and tail with one blow each. Mr. Segal's right arm, the one that held the machete-sized beheading knife, was much thicker than his left, the product of dispatching fish Mondays through Saturdays. My father's right arm and shoulder were similarly muscled from cutting meat.

Pushcarts lined the curbs for blocks like huge wheelbarrows with spoke wheels four feet in diameter and long shafts as if for horses. The carts rested on their smaller front wheels with the shafts angled skywards during business hours. They clogged the street so that there was just enough room for a single file of cars or a trolley to pass and fouled the curb with smell of rotting tomatoes, cabbage leaves and onions. In winter rusty fifty-five-gallon oil drums stood between some of the pushcarts with trash fires burning in them all day. The pushcart vendors stood round them for warmth until a customer appeared.

Mr. Drucker, a tall, thin, kindly-looking man, sold fruit and vegetables from his pushcart in front of the yarn store, and smiled at me and asked *Nu, Danela?* (*What's up, Danny?*) in Yiddish as I toddled by. He was there Monday through Saturday, no matter how hot or cold, and always wore a flat cloth cap. He could have been a pedlar in Lvov. At night Mr. Drucker closed up shop by levering onto the cart's shafts so his weight brought the front wheel off the cobbles as his feet hit the ground and the cart balanced on its two large wheels. Then with a heave he swung it from the curb, negotiated the trolley tracks and slowly pushed it round the corner and down three blocks to the pushcart garage where he locked it up for the night. The pushcarts, with their high wooden sides, steel-rimmed wooden wheels and goods, were heavy and didn't roll well. Moving them was a job for a horse, but Mr. Drucker had no horse.

Fourth Street was declining as a Jewish shopping district when my father bought the store in 1940. Jewish immigration from the Pale had been choked off in the twenties by the new US quota system and diminishing anti-Semitism that accompanied the first stages of Bolshevism in Russia. The first Jewish generation born in

Philadelphia prospered and promptly moved to better neighborhoods in Northeast and West Philadelphia. Poor blacks from the Southern states took their places, and with them came grinding poverty, different foods, more alcohol, violence and street crime. Rye bread, pickles, herring and corned beef gave way to hominy grits, collard greens, catfish and chitlins; the odor of garlic and cumin was replaced by the barbecue tang of wood smoke mixed with pig fat. At New Year Joe's Meats had wooden barrels four feet high and three wide with mounds of smoked hog jaws for sale, bristles and teeth still in them. This ghoulish food, roasted for hours with black-eyed peas and collard greens, was the traditional New Year's turkey for Southern field hands; it was supposed to bring luck.

There was a bar across the street and two hundred feet north of the store at the corner of Fourth and Bainbridge. Payday was Friday, and Friday and Saturday nights the sirens would wail their way to that bar; sometimes shots were heard, sometimes screams. Knife fights were common, as were back-alley crap games that ended violently. Many customers on Saturday and Sunday mornings were hung over, and it was not uncommon for the men to sport freshly bandaged hands and heads.

Joe sometimes ate lunch at Pearl's, a small luncheonette round the corner from the store. One Sunday we were sitting on stools at Pearl's counter eating lunch when a young black man said something which led the man, his companion and Joe to walk outside and square up. The tough pulled a nine-inch switchblade. Joe crouched, called him a nigger motherfucker and beat him to a pulp.

Joe's Meat Market would have failed ten years earlier than it did but for the coming of war. The U.S. Navy Yard at the foot of Broad Street, some four miles southeast of William Penn's hat, was working three shifts a day when the Japanese attacked Pearl Harbor on December 7th, 1941. Local woolen mills, machine shops, foundries soon followed suit. They drew laborers, many of them black, to the city; any capable man or woman in South Philadelphia who wanted steady work at good wages had it, including some of my relatives. And these workers bought their meat at Joe's. For the first time my father was making more than a living.

The U.S. government rationed meats and staples like coffee and sugar, which spawned a black market. They created a federal agency, the Office of Price Administration (O.P.A.), with inspectors to police the ration system and prevent profiteering; this drove black market prices higher. Joe struck a deal with a black market slaughterhouse to assure his supply of meat. He fetched it from the slaughterer's at night in a Chevy panel truck and unloaded it himself. Word got round that you could always get plenty of pork chops and roasts at Joe's without ration coupons.

Whitey, an O.P.A. inspector in his fifties, nearly six foot tall, fat and officious, walked into the store one Saturday morning when it was packed with customers come to buy meat without ration coupons. If anyone asked the price of a cut the butcher called out *Next!* and the shopper left meatless. Whitey asked to see the ration coupons for what was being sold.

South Philadelphia's ghetto streets – Jewish, Italian, Irish, Black – produced many good semi-pro boxers, and Joe was one of them. He was 29, fast, with an Eastern European peasant's arms and shoulders thickened from butchering; he could take a punch. He had little respect for authority and a Depression-era fear of anything that threatened his living. His uncontrollable temper was legendary. Joe asked Whitey to come back on Monday when the weekend rush was over. Whitey asked again, and Joe came from behind the counter, faced him and told him to come back another day. Whitey started to shut the front door, saying he would order the store closed if Joe didn't show him the coupons, and Joe knocked him through the front door's plate glass.

The Kevitch family lawyer defended Joe at his trial, which Uncle Abe attended to see justice done. When Whitey was called to the stand he rose, looked at Uncle Abe and said *Abe, if my dead mother got up from her grave and begged I wouldn't lift a finger to help that kid of yours*, then testified as damningly as he could. My father did not go to jail. He paid a modest fine; business went on as usual.

Joe began to teach his wife to drive shortly after they married, a time when trolleys ran frequently over the steel tracks in front of 716 South Fourth. The pre-war family coupe had a manual clutch and gearshift Louise found difficult to learn. She began to pull away from the curb one Sunday afternoon, my father in the passenger seat instructing, and stalled on the tracks. She flooded the carburetor trying to restart the car as a trolley, bell clanging, stopped inches from the coupe's back bumper. The starter turned the engine over futilely while the conductor continued to ring his bell for my mother to clear the tracks. After a minute or so he leaned from his window and cursed her, her sex, intelligence and parents. The passenger's door flew open and Joe ran to the trolley car, pried open the front double doors, dragged the conductor from the car and knocked him out. The conductor lay still on the cobbles as my father walked back to the car, got behind the wheel, started it and drove away.

A few days before Christmas 1946 Joe won $250, $2500 in today's money, in a crap game and blew it all on two sets of O-gauge Lionel model electric trains, passenger and freight, for my brother and me. Lionel did not manufacture model trains during the war and the first post-war sets were in short supply and very expensive. The freight set's six-wheel driver workhorse steam engine pulled a coal tender and silver Sunoco oil tanker, orange boxcar with Baby Ruth logo, operating black flatbed log car and a caboose. A sleek ten-wheel Pennsylvania Railroad passenger steam engine, with tender, rocketed three passenger cars and a club car round the layout, their windows lit by a bulb inside each car. Both engines puffed fake smoke after a white pellet dropped down their smokestacks melted on the hot headlight bulbs below. The whistle diaphragm was located in the tenders and activated by a button on a controller clipped to the track. Pressing a button on a remote controller would trigger a plunger on the track below the log car to tip the floor of the car up and dump the three toy logs it carried. Accessories included a gateman with a swinging lantern who popped out of his gatehouse when a train rolled over a nearby contact, a half dozen street lights and a transformer to run it all. Joe sat on the floor with a buddy in the front room above the store that Christmas morning assembling track and wiring controllers. He ran those trains round whistling and smoking all Christmas day, and every Christmas after, till I was twelve. My father had few toys as a child, and no trains. Sixty-five years later I still run them round at Christmas.

Early in 1946 Joe was diagnosed with Crohn's disease, an infection of the intestines that ultimately blocks the bowels. The famous surgeon who removed much of his rotted tripe in a pioneering operation saved his life — he left hospital weighing eighty-five pounds — and ordered him to convalesce and find a hobby. He went to Florida with Louise for his first vacation and there began to fish from a Miami pier as a form of therapy. By the time he returned from Florida he was hooked. A diversion became a passion, then an obsession and finally a calling: he died a charter captain on the Jersey coast. But his bowels and stomach tortured him the remaining forty-nine years of his life; he developed stomach cancer at eighty which would soon have killed him had a heart attack not carried him off first.

5141 Whitaker Ave

Stacks of $20, $50 and $100 bills with rubber bands around them, the four-year fruits of war, covered the kitchen table on V-J Day, August 15th, 1945, waiting to be hidden in a bank's safe deposit box. One year later Joe returned from convalescing in Florida, thirty-two years old, with a new-found passion for saltwater sport fishing, an even chance he would die young and the memory of signs at Southern hotels saying *No Jews or dogs allowed*. It was the worst possible time to buy a house; demand penned by the war, returning servicemen with G.I. loans, and wartime dearth of construction had inflated prices. But for the first time in my father's life a pigmy front lawn, grassy side plot in a private alleyway between the next row of two-story houses, finished basement with oak floors and a six-foot mahogany bar with three leather stools and a garage were his if he wanted them. So Joe took some stacks from the safe deposit box and bought an end-of-row house in Feltonville, a working- and lower-middle-class neighborhood in North Phila-delphia, to which we moved a few months before my fifth birthday. The house was never worth as much as it was that spring of 1947, and my parents lost most of their investment in real terms when they sold it forty years later.

Joe often visited the "box" over the next eight years. War work dwindled and with it went Fourth Street's shoppers. Every month my parents spent more than the store took in. Joe's innards continued to rot, his money worries worsened, Louise grew fat, and bickering became screaming matches with fists slamming tables and smashed plates. But Joe's visit to the *schvitz*, the local steam baths, each Monday of the year and his fishing trip each Tuesday, March through mid-December, Louise's "help," weekly beauty parlor and the family's annual two weeks at the "shore" – Atlantic City or Long Beach Island – continued. They borrowed money for emer-gencies and took the last cash stack from the "box" when I was twelve.

My parents used my fifth birthday to display their new house to the Burts and Kevitches. (When Uncle Bernie changed his name after the war from Jewish-sounding Bort to the WASP-ier Burt to help his career as a lingerie buyer for a downtown department store, Joe followed suit.) The Burt family war hero, Uncle Moishe, showed up, as did his Kevitch counterpart, Uncle Milton. Both had served in the Pacific, Milton as a military policeman, Moishe as a paratrooper. Milton brought home a Japanese rifle and malaria; Moishe, a chest of medals, a metal right arm and leg, chrome claw hand and an addiction to morphine acquired surviving wounds. He charged and destroyed an enemy machine-gun nest on Guadalcanal to earn medal, prostheses, pensions and federal benefits. Handsome, still dashing, Uncle Moishe married five times before he died, a successful chicken farmer, in Texas.

I met him for the first time that birthday and quickly told him about my Japanese rifle Uncle Milt had given me, which he asked to see. We went down to the basement, and when I showed it to him he picked it up with hand and claw, made me promise not to tell anyone, then taught me how to make a bayonet thrust. I saw him once more a few years later at Fourth and Daly when Joe would have beat him senseless had my grandparents not managed to drag him away. Moishe, the youngest of their four children and Mom's favorite, had persuaded them to mortgage their house to fund a business deal. The deal, if there had been a deal, went south, leaving Mom and Pop with a mortgage they couldn't pay, Pop dying and no other assets to speak of. We went to their house ostensibly for my father to discuss what was to be done, but when he saw Moishe he lost his temper and punched him. I never saw or heard from Moishe again; he did not attend either of his parents' funerals, nor my father's. He had numerous children, my cousins, whom I have never met, whose names I have never known.

The new house in Feltonville had a "breakfast room" where we ate at a table seating six, separated by a half wall from a small kitchen, the last of five modest rooms on the first floor. Joe sat at the head of the table on the two or three nights a week when he was home early enough for us to eat as a family. If he was not present, his chair stayed empty, as did the large red-plush armchair with thick feather-stuffed cushions in the living room. We were forbidden to sit in it after the cushions were plumped in the evening for his return from work.

There was no art or pictures on the walls, no musical instruments.

Volumes of the *Reader's Digest Condensed Book Club*, a set of *Encyclopedia Britannica* and *The Naked and the Dead* stood on four shelves in the basement. Our periodicals were *Reader's Digest*, *Life*, *Look*, *Vogue* and *Salt Water Sportsman*. A television rested on the living room's "wall-to-wall" carpet. There was a large pre-war 78 Victrola-cum-radio with amber-colored tuning face on a shelf in the basement above a small stack of "swing" and "big band" records from the forties, one of which contained Al Jolsen singing "The Anniversary Waltz." The first two lines Jolsen sang go: "Oh how we danced on the night we were wed / we vowed our true love though a word wasn't said," which Joe regularly rendered in a loud baritone as "Oh how we danced on the night we were wed / I needed a wife like a hole in the head." Linoleum covered the breakfast room and kitchen floors.

The door slammed behind him when he came home, visibly tired, and called out *Lou, is dinner ready?* They did not greet each other, nor kiss, nor touch. I never saw them kiss. If dinner was late a fight would start. Joe generally ate dinner alone, reading the paper. At breakfast he would go over yesterday's receipts and lists of provisions to be picked up at wholesalers. When the family ate together he talked to his sons rather than to his wife. If he spoke to her at table it was often about how bad business had been that day or week or month. After dinner he flopped in his chair to read the paper, smoke a cigarette and doze off. He went upstairs to bed around ten.

Louise did not go with him. She sat watching television in the living room, or in the kitchen talking on the telephone, drinking coffee, smoking and doodling on scraps of paper and newspaper margins. After half an hour or so he would call *Lou, Lou, come to bed*. Most mornings I found her asleep on the couch in the living room. They shared a bedroom, but she rarely slept in it when he was in the bed. He was consistently unfaithful to her their entire wedded lives, either with whores or with girlfriends. One affair she suspected must have worried her more than most, because she set her brother to catch him. A scene followed when she presented the evidence in front of us children. He began to pack, she kept berating him, dishes flew, and she threatened to call her brother Albert. Joe never hit her. In time their marriage decayed into indifference, his excuse for not leaving *you kids*, hers *how would I support myself* and *what would people say*.

The day began with screams and shouts. Our house had one

bathroom for the four of us with tile floor, single sink, shower and tub, and a basement W.C. A maid came three days a week, we had a washing machine and later a dryer, but clean clothes often shirked the climb from basement laundry room to bedrooms. Mornings were a scramble to empty bowels and bladders, find clean underwear and socks and get to work or school; the house rang with cries of *Lou, where's my shorts?* or *Mom, I need socks*. Yesterday's dinner dishes tilted at odd angles in a yellow rubber-coated drying rack by the kitchen sink where unwashed pots with last night's congealed rice or potatoes were piled.

Pop died in 1954 and Mom turned her *kvetching* (corrosive whining) on her children and their wives. She always worried about money, though between her social security checks and her children's help she had more than enough, and used a "limited" phone service. This allowed her two free calls a day for a nominal fee. She husbanded her free calls for "emergencies" and signaled with two rings when she wanted family to call her. Her signals became a ukase, ignored at your peril.

Mom "signaled" almost every evening before Joe came home, while Louise was struggling to fix supper. Apparently bearing two sons, time and self-interest had cleansed the *shiksa* from Louise's blood. If Louise didn't ring back immediately, Mom would use one of her "emergency" calls to complain to Joe when he came home from work. Dinner was never on time; asked when it would be ready, Louise snapped, *When I say so*. We ate hostage to the signal. Mom died at 99 and lived alone until her death.

The neighborhood was about sixty percent Gentile and forty percent Jewish when we moved to Feltonville, but the Jews were leaving for the suburbs. It was seventy percent Gentile by the time I was twelve and today is an Hispanic section of Philadelphia's inner city. The Catholic kids mostly went to Saint Ambrose Parochial School on Roosevelt Boulevard. Saint Ambrose was attached to a large Catholic church in the next block west from our synagogue. Fights with the Saint Ambrosians were a staple of the Jewish High Holy Days. It was generally accepted that the Gentile boys, the *shcutz*, were tougher than the Jewish, with a few exceptions.

Creighton Elementary was the local public primary school, teaching grades kindergarten through eight. It was a four-story ochre brick building set on a third of a city block. An adjoining concrete schoolyard and a gravel playing field occupied the rest. Six-foot-high pointy iron palings set three inches apart formed a palisade from the school's north façade round the cement schoolyard and gravel ball field to the building's south façade. There were heavy steel mesh grilles painted off-white on the ground-level windows. It looked like a prison. The gates were locked from 4 p.m. to 7:30 the next morning. There were an assembly hall where every morning we said a prayer, pledged allegiance to the flag and heard a reading, sometimes from the Old but mostly from the New Testament; an oak-floored gym half again the size of a basketball court with several vaulting horses, sweat-gray tattered tumbling mats, rings, climbing ropes to the ceilings and two basketball hoops at either end; a wood shop where sixth-, seventh- and eighth-grade boys learned to handle the tools they would need for adult jobs, and made "zip guns;" and a "Home Ec" room with stoves, refrigerators and sewing machines where girls learned the skills of their sex. Thanksgiving, Christmas and Easter were the big holidays, with paper turkeys, crèches, dyed eggs, bunnies and baskets in profusion. Few Old Creightonians went to college.

Our neighborhood was roughly eight blocks long and four deep, bounded on the north by the Boulevard, on the east by railroad tracks, south by a creek where we trapped tadpoles and west by the Boulevard again. It supported eleven "mom and pop stores" on eleven corners: two groceries, two kosher butchers, two candy stores, a corner drug store, barber shop, beauty parlor, shoe repair, and Polan's, a luncheonette. The northeastern U.S. headquarters of catalog retailer Sears Roebuck, with a two-square block, three-story department store attached, was four blocks away across the Boulevard. The department store entrance housed a popcorn machine and vendor selling large bags of it for 15¢. A baseball, knife, deflated football or basketball fit neatly below the popcorn at the bottom of one of these bags, and the advent of spring and fall found groups of boys wandering the sporting goods aisles munching popcorn and looking out for store detectives.

We played on Whitaker Avenue's wide asphalt street, a six-blocks-long dead-end stretch. There were no parks or playgrounds. Boys played stick-ball with a cut-off broom handle for bat and a hollow rubber ball two and a quarter inches in diameter; half-ball with the same bat but the ball cut in half and inverted so it looked like a deep saucer and dipped, curved and floated unpredictably when properly pitched; and hose-ball, again with the same broom-handle bats and four-inch lengths of rubber cut from garden hoses. Sensible neighbors kept their brooms and hoses inside from Easter until the players had stolen enough of both for the coming season. The street game from September till Christmas was rough touch American football. Participants left these games cut and bruised from slamming into parked cars and curbs, sometimes with sprains, occasionally with a broken arm or leg. The parked cars did not fare well either. There was a stop sign where a side street from the Boulevard intersected Whitaker Avenue. Joe drove down that street every day when he came home from work, but never stopped. The neighbors cursed him in fear for their children and themselves.

Competition from the national food chains, A&P and Food Fair, and the Jewish exodus were slowly throttling the local stores, except for Polan's, where the Jewish *gonifs* (hustlers) hung out. Every Monday night between seven and eight they gathered to settle the weekend's gambling debts. Accounts were settled when "Fats," a 350-pound man in his late thirties, and his two bodyguards drove off in his white Cadillac convertible. One afternoon drink-fuelled insults – "kike" and "sheeny" – from mourners at an Irish wake a few doors from Polan's led to shoving, a *hey rube!* and brawl, followed by police and ambulances. The guys who hung out at Polan's were not sissies, and the grade school boys there eating hamburgers and fries looked up to them.

Joe worked five and a half days a week, fishing and *schvitz* his only recreation. The store was open every day except for national holidays like Christmas and Easter Sunday, and he had only one helper. He was too tired or worried to talk much when he came home from work; he never encouraged anyone to become a butcher. During our two-week holiday at the "shore" in August, he arrived from Philadelphia late on Sunday night, spent Monday afternoon with us on the beach and returned to Philadelphia after fishing Tuesday. The one vacation he took was a fishing trip to Cape Hatteras, North Carolina, for channel bass, five years after his convalescence, with me along.

Hatteras is ten hours southeast by car and ferry from Philadelphia. We arrived at a motel near Ocracoke Inlet, North Carolina, at two in the morning in the middle of a nor'easter. It was still blowing hard four hours later when we woke to seas too rough to fish. A grand old wooden resort hotel just opening for the season was recommended for breakfast. There was one table in use in the otherwise closed dining room. We were seated with another party of breakfasting fishermen from Philadelphia at the long table; Joe knew one of them. A tall, courtly, white-haired black waiter was serving. He took our order, and ham, bacon, eggs arrived in due course, with large sides of hominy grits, a ground maize porridge served slathered in butter, a staple of Southern breakfasts.

North Carolina had been a slave state and a lynchpin of the Confederacy. Segregation, *de jure* and *de facto*, was the ironclad rule in 1952, two years before the U.S. Supreme Court ruled segregated schooling illegal. The Klan was large and powerful; the washrooms, restaurants, water fountains and motels separate, and blacks rode in the back of the bus. Jews were little more popular.

The other party finished before us and one of them called to the waiter, *Boy! Boy! Cum y'ere*, in an ersatz, mocking, field hand's patois from *Gone with the Wind*. The waiter approached: *Yes sir, can I help you?* The man replied *Boy, dem's was rail fahn grits. Why's, dey's de bestest grits ah evah did have! Could ah's have's some more of dem dere grits?* The waiter said, *I'm glad you liked them, sir. I'll check with the kitchen.* The bigot sat down, smirking, and the waiter headed for the kitchen. My father rose, plate in hand, before the waiter took two steps, walked round and scraped his grits onto the man's plate, saying *Here, you want some more grits?* Joe stood beside him while the man ate the grits; the waiter looked on from the side of the room.

Joe did only two things religiously: fished each Tuesday from March till mid-December and went to *schvitz* on Mondays. His aging mother he saw once or twice a month when her nagging made him feel guilty; he visited his brother-in-law with the family at Christmas, met cousins-in-law if there was a problem or at a crap game, went to a movie, dinner or family celebration three or four times a year with his wife, and worked the rest of the time. His stomach troubles had stopped his serious drinking in '47, and he generally whored discreetly.

The *schvitz* was the Camac Baths, a three-story building half a block square built almost to the curb on Camac Street, an alley eight minutes' walk southeast from City Hall. A clerk stood behind a desk in the small foyer in front of rows of steel lock boxes with keys on elastic wristbands hanging from their little doors, behind which steel trays a foot long with two-inch-high sides all round rested in cubbies. The clerk gave you one of these trays for your valuables as you signed in. Joe always carried a wad of cash two or three inches thick, which he placed with his wallet and watch in the tray and watched the clerk lock it in its cubby hole. The clerk handed you the key to the lock box, a bed sheet and paper bath shoes, and you went through another door on your right into the locker room.

The locker room was a well lighted, forty-foot-square space smelling of liniment and disinfectant, with tiled floor and several hundred sheet metal hanging lockers arranged in facing rows of thirty with benches between them. There was also a barber shop, shoe-shine stand, cafeteria, and "sun room" for tanning. You undressed, draped the sheet over yourself like a toga, called *Locker* for an attendant to lock up your clothes and shuffled through another door and down a staircase to the baths. Along the far perimeter of the basement that housed the baths were two twelve-by-eighteen-foot white tiled hot rooms behind two plate glass doors; towel-draped deck chairs lined their walls. The temperature in one was 125, the other 150 degrees Fahrenheit. A ten-by-ten-foot steam room reeking of pine adjoined the cooler hot room. Marble benches lined its walls and there was a cold shower in the corner to cool down in order to prolong the time you could bear the steam.

At the other end of the baths was the *platza* room where the *platza* man, naked except for a black canvas loincloth, cold water coursing down him from a hose stuffed under a floppy canvas hat he wore, rubbed you down with soapy brushes fashioned from euca-lyptus leaves. Joe always "took" a *platza*. He would lie on the highest of the room's three oak racks with a canvas hat fished from a bucket of cold water on his head, Willie the *platza* man, six-one and a good 230 pounds, looming over him. Willie controlled the heat from a lever under the second level of benches; each time he depressed it the room got hotter. Joe viewed a *platza* as a contest between him and Willie to see who would quit first. Willie had the insuperable advantage of standing in the cold water shower from the hose under his hat and could give *platzas* for hours. He would bear down on you with the brush, massaging, washing and cooking you at the same time. Every three or four minutes he would ratchet up the heat, and once in a while take the hose from under his hat and sprinkle your most tender parts, like the backs of your calves, with cold water. Joe drove out anyone else taking a *platza* when he took his; once even Willie wilted.

Finished, Willie helped you down from the *platza* bench and into the stall immediately outside for a cold shower. He handed his favorites a shot of bourbon from a pint bottle secreted in the *platza* room and then they went for their "sheet wrap." Twelve or so deck chairs stood along rails forming a twelve-by-twelve-foot square between the *platza* and the hot rooms. An attendant covered a deck chair with towels and a sheet and you reclined in it. He laid towels across your chest, legs, and arms, swathed your head and neck in more, and wrapped the sheet around you like tinfoil round a roast. There you lay, sweating and dozing or talking to other shrouded men.

The Camac Baths transplanted to America an Eastern European ritual from the Pale. Camac's mid-century habitués were mostly men who did heavy labor, frequently out of doors – butchers, fish-mongers, poultry men, pushcart men who sold clothes, fruit, and vegetables, knife grinders, rag and bone men, sheet metal workers, carpenters like Zaida, plumbers, painters, the panoply of working-class trades from the *shtetls*: aging immigrants and their first-generation sons. They came to Camac to get fat, grease, gristle and grime out of their skins and in winter the cold out of their bones. The older men spoke Yiddish and English, as my father did, frequently switching from one to the other mid-sentence; the younger men talked in English. Imprecations and curses were almost always in Yiddish. The second generation moved away and Camac closed in the late 'eighties.

Aaron Wildavsky was a butcher nearly six and a half feet tall with hawser arms, bollard legs and a surprisingly mild disposition. One day after a *platza*, while the two men lay near each other wrapped in sheets, Joe got into an argument with him about why Eastern Europe's Jews went meekly to their deaths. Aaron's mother tongue was Yiddish and he slipped into it more and more often as he tried to counter Joe's incredulity and contempt. He kept saying *Yossel, Yossel, du fa'shtaisht nisht, du fa'shtaisht nisht* (Joe, Joe, you don't understand, you don't understand), and told him the ruses, reasons and overwhelming force the Nazis used. When Aaron rose to shower and loosed his sheets, I noticed faded black numbers on his left forearm. At the time I thought my father had been unspeakably cruel; now I think he was scared.

News boys hawked the evening dailies between lanes of traffic on the Boulevard when Joe drove home from work or *schvitz*, and he always tried to time the lights so he could buy a paper from them. In winter or when it rained he always bought a paper from them, even if the lights were green.

Pennsauken

Childhood's venues faded at twelve when I went to work in the Pennsauken Merchandise Mart, a windowless "farmers' market" on forty level acres in New Jersey five minutes across the Delaware River from Philadelphia. Joe bought a half interest in a butcher shop there after he closed his failing Fourth Street store, and, to save money, put me to work in its cutting room and on its counter selling meat. The Mart was a one-story, flat-roofed, yellow cinderblock coffin floating in an open sea of asphalt where a thousand cars could park. Five blocks long, two boxcars wide, it took more than ten minutes to walk one of its two aisles end to end. Customers, almost all of whom were working-class or poor, entered through eight steel double doors evenly spaced down its two long sides, or the double glass doors at either end. It had no windows or skylights; once inside, whether it was night or day, fair or foul became a mystery, except when hail or heavy rain thrummed on the sheet metal roof.

You could hear rats – we called them freezer rats – scuttle away when you opened the door to the large walk-in freezer opposite the cutting room. They gnawed through a foot of concrete foundation and three-inch plywood floor to nibble frozen turkeys stored for the holidays. We shaved the chewed portions with a bandsaw to remove their teethmarks before the turkeys went on sale. You could smell rancid grease and green pork scraps, as well as sage mixed with sodium nitrite to turn all pink again, when we made sausage. You could see heat rise in waves from the asphalt parking lot, the Mart shimmer, when the temperature hit one hundred degrees in summer, and feel the tar suck your shoes down as you walked across the melting parking lot. But you could not see, or smell, or hear childhood any longer.

3. Other Worlds

Barnegat

Long Beach Island is an eighteen-mile sand spit facing the Atlantic Ocean which Barnegat Bay splits from the New Jersey pine barrens.

The narrow island is pancake flat except for a sand dune spine one-story high down its entire length a few hundred feet back from the surf: the ocean cut it in two at least three times in the last century during spring nor'easters. It has clean beach margins for vacationers and the best fishing in Jersey out of Barnegat Light. Joe fished its bays, inlets and offshore waters from the time I was four and a half.

The sea is a perilous place. I went down to it for the first time in late spring 1947. My father and I, plus a nurse for him "just in case," boarded a charter boat at Beach Haven to fish for flounder. A charter boat, booked in advance, fishes for whatever the "party" wants, unlike the much cheaper "head boats" that take all comers at so much a head to fish for what's advertised. We were catching flounder when the captain told us to reel in and made for a distress flare from a U-Drive garvey drifting half a mile away.

Tyros could rent small boats like garveys to run themselves – "U-Drives" – for the day. The drive shaft came out the back end of an engine box mounted on deck amidships and down through the deck to form a small triangle covered by a wooden housing. Nothing covered this garvey's drive shaft: when the engine ran, the shaft and propeller coupling rotated unprotected above the deck. One of the men aboard her had caught his trouser cuff in the turning coupling, shredding his leg from ankle to knee. There was blood everywhere – I saw the man's shin bone white through his flesh before my father bundled me away – and he was screaming. Our nurse bandaged his tatters, gave him a shot of morphine from a first aid kit and we waited for the coastguard.

Holmes Russell ran parties on his garvey in 1947 to fish for striped bass and bluefish in-shore. He was a North Carolinian from a hillbilly family, wiry, white-haired and missing three fingertips, two from his left, one from his right hand. Sun and salt water had tanned his skin almost to leather. Holmes, or "Russ" as Joe called him, grew up on the waters round Oregon Inlet, ran a still in the Carolina Blue Ridge Mountains during Prohibition, and delivered white lightning to the towns below. He could fix anything, built his own thirty-six-foot fishing boat named the *Jolly Roger* as well as his house at Barnegat Light, and was reputed the best in-shore skipper on the Jersey coast. He used the garvey to catch grass shrimp for bait and to clam in winter. The garvey was battleship gray; on a rainy December afternoon, bent over its side jamming a pair of long-handled clamming tongs into the Barnegat mud flats, he and it seemed wraiths.

Joe began chartering with Holmes when Holmes still fished from the garvey. Striped bass are a prized in-shore game fish: wily, hard-fighting and weighing up to eighty pounds, their white, dry flesh especially good eating. Holmes knew more about them and how to catch them than anyone else. They wintered in brackish creeks that feed Barnegat Bay, and in the spring schools of three- to five-pounders, *schoolies*, headed down the Bay and out the Inlet to feed on sand eels offshore and migrate north. Bigger fish haunted the jetties and bars of the Barnegat Inlet from spring through late fall; if you wanted big bass it was the Inlet you fished to catch them.

The shoals which stud the east coast's inlets south of Cape Cod make them treacherous gauntlets in an onshore wind: Barnegat Inlet is one of the worst. A tiara of sand bars rings it from north to south, and sand bar pendants choke its approaches. Dutch settlers named it *Barendegat*, "inlet of the breakers," in 1614, for the seas that rear meerschaum white and break over its bars in the calmest weather. The Inlet is impassable when strong easterly winds pile seas on its bars. There is always a boom and roar of waves breaking; close up they sound like rushing trains. Lines from "The Charge of the Light Brigade" come to mind as you round the Barnegat Light House and head east towards the breaking seas:

Cannon to right of them
Cannon to left of them
Cannon in front of them
      Volly'd and thunder'd

For nearly a century and a half men tried to tame the Inlet. The Army Corps of Engineers built two gray granite boulder jetties in the early 1900s from the Inlet's north and south shores, like a half-mile-long rock funnel, to channel water from bay to ocean and stop the north tip of Long Beach Island from eroding. The Corps had no more success than Canute; the bars continued to grow, shrink, and shift, and the Island's sands washed away. The Corps beefed them up with more rocks every fifteen years or so, to no avail. The U.S. Life Saving Service opened station #17 at the Light around 1872; the coastguard has a well manned station there to this day. A thirty-five-foot coastguard lifeboat, double-ended like a great white canoe with a wheelhouse in its middle, always lay in the Inlet in rough weather to rescue boats in trouble. She had two powerful engines and could roll through 360 degrees, right herself and stay on station. Nevertheless one or two boats got in trouble in the Inlet every year, and one or more men were lost. Few amateurs used the Barnegat Inlet in the fifties.

I was six my first time in the Inlet. Joe had chartered Captain Jack Sylvester's twenty-eight-foot skiff to troll for blues offshore. The mate was Sylvester's twelve-year-old son Barty. A storm had passed offshore a few days earlier and big swells were running. They made up into breaking seas higher than the skiff's cabin top when they fetched up on the bars. The coastguard lifeboat rolled wildly on station at the in-shore edge of the north bar. Sylvester had a drink problem and may not have been quite clear-headed enough that morning to realize it was not a good day to take a skiff through the Inlet, or perhaps he was desperate for his hire. We were a third of the way out of the Inlet, taking big seas on the bow every few minutes, by the time he decided to quit, but turning back was dangerous. Barty went below and came up with life jackets, big bulky yellow pre-war canvas vests with cork blocks sewn in pockets for flotation. Joe helped me into mine and tied it tight. The critical moment would come when Sylvester tried to go about and we would be sideways to the waves rather than with our nose into them. If a sea caught us broadside to we could capsize.

Joe cut an eight-foot length of rope and tied one end round his waist and another round my left ankle. As Sylvester prepared to put the wheel over my father looked at me and said, *Whatever happens, don't let go of the rope.* He had beat me, he had yelled at me, but never had he told me to do anything the way he told me to hold on to that rope. We came about in the trough of a sea, and, pitching and rolling, scuttled safely back through the Inlet. That was Joe's last trip with Sylvester, who left Barnegat and his family not long after. Holmes married Sylvester's ex-wife; Barty became his stepson and the *Jolly Roger*'s mate.

The favored ways to catch stripers, requiring the most skill and with the greatest chance of catching a large one, were to chum the jetties or cast the bars. Inch-and-a-half-long grass shrimp with shells the color of the sandy bottom where they lived made the Barnegat jetties a buffet for stripers. Holmes would anchor within ten feet of their rocks so that a rivulet of chum, four or five grass shrimp sprinkled from a live bait box every few minutes, trickled down the jetty from the boat. Light lines with two shrimp impaled on little black hooks floated along with the chum. There is an art to chumming: Holmes explained it to Joe the first time they anchored on the jetty – how to bait the hook, strip the line, what the trick was – then stood beside him and started catching bass. After baiting, stripping and going fishless for an hour while Holmes caught bass after bass, Joe asked him to explain again. Homes said, *I showed you once; watch me.* Joe never asked again: he fished next to Holmes for a year and a half before he caught his first bass. Most men can remember when, where and with whom they caught theirs; I was eleven, chumming on the inside of the north jetty with Holmes.

It was a fair fight between angler and striper on the jetties: one had tackle, skill, a boat; the other, strength, sea and rocks. Big bass head for the open sea when they're hooked. You can't stop them with light chumming tackle, and a fish much over twenty pounds runs until it tires of fighting the rod tip and reel drag. Joe and Holmes were chumming inside the south jetty in the garvey at high tide in early spring when Joe hooked a bass he couldn't slow, a fish more powerful than any he'd hooked before. It steamed across the jetty bound for Ireland and soon would either strip the reel or cut the line on the jetty's barnacles. Joe hollered *Russ, I can't hold him* and Holmes yelled back *Hold on!* Net boats had caught some very large bass offshore a few days before and Holmes had visions of a light tackle world record. He started the engine, cut the anchor line and eyed the seas washing over the jetty. He picked a big one, gunned the garvey toward the rocks, cleared them and chased that bass into the open sea with Joe in the bow, rod tip high, reeling when the bass paused. They were nearly two miles at sea ninety minutes later when Holmes gaffed the striper. Not a record, but not many pounds shy.

The *Jolly Roger* lay in the wash of six- to eight-foot-high seas break-ing across the north bar on a fall afternoon, her party casting with light spinning tackle for bass. Joe hooked one too strong to turn that headed for deep water beyond the bar. The only chance to land it was to follow it through the breakers into deep water. Holmes reversed the engine and backed down across the bar. The cockpit swamped, but Holmes kept going. When Joe stood beside the sixty-pound bass for photographs that evening, someone asked him why he was wet almost to his armpits.

Holmes rarely cast off more than a half-hour past sunrise; if one of the party was late he didn't fish with Russ that day. Barnegat Light was a ninety-minute drive from Whitaker Avenue down a two-lane highway, so Joe often left before 4 a.m. One morning he overslept and had under an hour before the *Jolly Roger* sailed when he started his new 1954 Chrysler Windsor. A state trooper fell in behind him as he accelerated east from the last circle down Route 72. He saw the flashing light, heard the siren and held the hammer down. The chase continued at a steady 100 to 115 miles an hour, as fast as that Chrysler went, for thirty miles down 72, across the causeway onto the Island and north to the dock, where Holmes had the engine running and all but one mooring line untied. Joe screeched into the parking lot and the trooper roared in behind. Joe leaped from the car, ran the few feet to the boat, jumped aboard and Holmes cast off. They had a good day. Two state police cruisers and four troopers were waiting on the dock to arrest Joe when the *Jolly Roger* backed into her slip that afternoon.

Heavy black rubber bags filled with iced fluke, stripers and weak-fish in spring and fall, and blues, tuna and stripers in summer, rode home with Joe from the Tuesday fishing trip. Neighbors watched his car roll up our alley and hoped he'd had a good day. They came with newspaper under their arms to ask if he had fish for them. He dumped the catch, ice, blood and melt on the cement by our back drain, hosed it down and gave away what we didn't need, often most of what lay on the ground. He washed, rinsed and left the bags to dry in the garage until next Monday night when he loaded the car again with rods, reels, and tackle for the pre-dawn drive to Barnegat Light. The alley smelled of fish on Wednesday mornings and local trash cans brimmed with fish heads, tails and scales wrapped in old newspapers.

Holmes and Joe fished together for eight years. After Holmes built the *Jolly Roger*, and over-fishing had decimated bass stocks, they abandoned the jetties for offshore: the Barnegat Ridge for blues on spinning tackle till hands were too tired to turn the reel cranks, the ocean beyond for tuna up to 100 pounds, 150-pound mako sharks and a white marlin or two. But the *Jolly Roger* was slow, and Holmes' *forte* was not blue-water work beyond the Ridge, where charts, parallel rulers, compasses and protractors were needed; he never was quite comfortable further offshore than dead reckoning could take him. It was long before the days of G.P.S. and Holmes' reading was a little uncertain. Joe learned almost all Holmes had to teach him about the sea and fishing.

Ducks and geese rose quacking and honking out of the bay's salt-marshes at daybreak as the charter boats headed for the Inlet. Ribbons of them streaked the skies, heading north in spring and south in fall. Clouds of gulls wheeled above the bars and beyond the breakers off the beaches and dove on fleeing bait fish. The sun rose like a new penny from the sea's edge as we'd head offshore; helmsmen squinted into it to avoid flotsam and keep their course. It died rose red and blinded them again heading home. White caps form when the wind rises above ten knots and the sea backs glow mint green. Beyond the sixty-fathom line ocean turns magnolia green. At sea there were no vomiting drunks, no aprons with rust-brown dried pork blood, no customers demanding cuts from the front of the case, no cops on the take, no rats behind rice sacks, no registers, no pushcart men and boys huddled round oil drum trash fires waiting for trade. There were no Jews remembering pogroms, no hit men, no bullies. Barnegat Light was his Blessed Isles, and Joe fell in love with the sea.

After a few years, fishing one day a week was too little; Joe began to fish Wednesdays as well and muse on the long pre-dawn drives to the dock about buying a boat and becoming a charter captain. Holmes was hardly encouraging and other charter-men told him he had too much to learn before he could handle a boat in the Inlet and fish the waters offshore, that he was too choleric to make a skipper. He bought a twenty-five-foot single-engine Maycraft early one summer in the mid-fifties, named her *Dan-Rick* after his two sons in the order of their birth, and a week later took her tuna fishing. He was forty miles off when the prevailing southwesterly built to twenty miles an hour from ten, as it will on a summer afternoon, and what had been a following sea became a head sea when he came about for home. The course back was almost dead into the wind and a five-foot sea: it was four hours going and eight coming back. He took more water over the bow than ever he did again and was soaked through when he reached the dock, shaken, aware the *Dan-Rick* would not serve his purpose.

Seamen say that thirty foot and over it's the skipper not the boat that counts. The Maycraft was gone within days, replaced by a thirty-foot Pacemaker with twin ninety-five-horsepower Chrysler engines, carvel-planked and soft-chined. She rolled but didn't pound and made her way featly through a head sea. It's supposedly bad luck to change a boat's name; he christened the Pacemaker *Dan-*

Rick and so she remained. His third boat and then his last were *Dan-Ricks*, too. Joe took friends fishing on *Dan-Rick* for a few years with me as mate and began to study for a charter captain's license to take people fishing for hire. He was known as Captain Joe when he died forty years later in 1995, the only Jewish charter captain on the Jersey coast. Some said he was as good as was Holmes in his prime, but I had been gone too long to attest to that. We buried him in his fishing clothes, *Capt. J. Burt* in blue thread script stitched across the left breast pocket of his short-sleeved khaki shirt, *Dan-Rick* across the right.

We fetched the second *Dan-Rick* from the Pacemaker yard at Forked River on a gray, windy late summer's morning. Thirty-five minutes later we were leaving the channel opposite the Barnegat Lighthouse when Joe decided to try her in a sea and headed east toward the south jetty rather than west to our dock. A palisade of breaking seas stretched in a concave arc from jetty to jetty beyond the Inlet's mouth, like a shark's jaw. The coastguard lifeboat rolled on the north bar; there were no boats offshore. Two boat lengths off the rocks and halfway up the south jetty it was clear that it was too rough to leave the Inlet. Joe put the wheel over to port to come about, but nothing happened. He twirled the wheel to starboard, but she did not answer. We had lost our steering in the inshore approach to the Barnegat Inlet in a twenty-five-mile-an-hour northeast wind. Joe grabbed the ship to shore's handset, tuned the dial to the distress channel, and I heard the first and so far only *Mayday! Mayday! Mayday!* from a vessel I was aboard. The Barnegat Light coastguard station answered and told us to anchor up and wait for the rescue boat; it was already underway. I went forward, untied the anchors and threw and set them both.

The coastguard towed us to their station, where a young coast-guardsman came aboard and helped us fix the steering. The *Dan-Rick* left the station at about 1:00 pm; we'd been there an hour. The wind had strengthened; rain squalls blew through from time to time, hiding the saltmarsh sedge the gusts bent almost double. Joe sat on the bridge in the wind and rain and, when we reached the channel a hundred yards or so from the station, turned toward the Inlet rather than our dock. We rounded the Lighthouse into the Inlet's approaches and picked up speed heading seaward. I called up *Hey, Dad, where you going?*; no answer. He was hunched stiff over the wheel, right hand on the twin throttles, long-billed fishing cap pulled low over his crewcut to keep out rain and occasional spray. Twelve-foot waves built and crashed in the channel as we slammed past the tower at the end of the south jetty.

Breaking seas in the Inlet come in sets. Captains hold their boats just short of where they break, backing down if necessary (reversing to let the seas break in front of them), and count seas waiting for a lull. When the last sea breaks the water beyond is white with foam but flat for half the length of a soccer pitch, and a boat can cross where the waves make up before the first sea in the next set builds. The *Dan-Rick* was new and fast for her day. Joe shouted from the bridge *Hold on!* and jammed the throttles all the way forward when a last sea broke. We skittered across a white foam tabletop through brown spots churned from the sand bar four or five feet below, swerved right toward the south bar to avoid a sea making up, took a small wave bow on and burst into the white-capped open ocean. Joe sat silent on the bridge.

We circled north outside the bars and reached the north jetty about halfway down from the tower at its seaward end. The north bar is shallower than the others, the seas steeper but not so wide, more dangerous if you're caught, but narrower seas to catch you. In a blow the professionals always went in the north side. They'd sneak up alongside the north jetty almost to the tower, keeping as close to the rocks as possible, wait for a lull, turn the bow into the bar and head across the mouth of the Inlet. When the next sea made up they turned right, got on its back and rode it like a surfboard shorewards toward the south jetty. Timed right, they were inside the bar safe home when it broke; too fast, and they overran the sea and pitch-poled; too slow and the following sea pooped them. Once committed you cannot stop. A coastguardsman in a life jacket watched through binoculars from the lifeboat as Joe began his run. He turned into the bar, opened her up, caught the next rising sea and rode its back across the shoal till it collapsed well down the south jetty.

I climbed the ladder to the bridge and sat beside him for the short run to the dock. He throttled back near the marina so our wake did not disturb boats tied there. I started down the ladder from the bridge to handle the bow lines when he said, without looking at me, *You know, Danny, if I hadn't done that I'd have never fished again.* I knew.

London

I live in London now, my countrymen are Britons. Wolfe maintained you can't go home again, literally true in my case. All but two of the men and women who figure in the stories you just read are dead. Three of the worlds are gone, the last changed utterly. What will happen to me is certain; I will die. It would be coy to say the trip has not been colorful, exciting at times, at times played on a public stage, but those are memories for friends and above all for a beloved. The "I" claims less attention towards life's end.

What does interest me is how vision forms, how I come to understand what I do of the world and whether that understanding is sound. The people and places described here, with one unloved exception, were not fantasists. I have tried to suggest how I came to my vision by recalling them and their countries, streets, waters and stories as clearly as I could. I revisited Fourth & Daly, Ninth & Race and all the rest. I did not visit Ukraine, where there are no more *shtetls*.

Childhood did not teach me how to behave or what to do in the world I live in. Except for one who loved me well, none imagined I would become a writer; now that I have, some ask why. My father would understand; he knew we all must run our inlets or know that we have failed.

III

Circumcision

*During the Second World War the Nazis often forced men
to drop their pants, to check if they were circumcised.*

Telushkin, *Jewish Literacy*

Father, grandfathers, great-grandfather stand
Round their issue soon to suffer rescission
In an ancient blood rite that leaves a band
Of scar and an heir by diminution.
By the door the women of the families
Stand, chattering until their cue to leave
When the knife appears, sugared brandy's
Poured, and talliths cover heads and sleeves.
To dull the pain from the approaching snip
The mohel soaks his finger in the brandy pap
Then gives it as a teat to the initiate
Lying turtled on great-grandpa's lap.
        A wrist flicks, a forebear leans to say
        For him our suffering began today.

Indices

Measurement began braced against a kitchen jamb,
Head back, neck stretched like a young giraffe
Nibbling high leaves, waiting for the hand
Flattening my hair to notch my wooden graph,
And swelled into a hunger no nicked door
Could sate. I shrank each milestone to size –
Schools and labours, lusts and loves – and scored
Them by league tables: money, conquests, wives;
A life, quantified.

                    Body marks me now
And I've had my fill of scores; but phthisis,
Shrinking bones, slack shank and jowl
Post the path to childhood's antithesis
No child can conceive, when with delight
It toddles toward evaluation and goodnight.

Inquisition

Sundays they trudged to the downtown *schvitz*,
An old trade rite, to steam suet and grit
From grimy pores and from bones the chill of
Ice-boxes and concrete floors. *Platzas*
Done, mummy-wrapped in cheap thin sheets
Flung over deck chairs from headrests to feet,
They rest in rows like corpses gathered
After a Cossack raid on the Dnieper.

It could have been Odessa, before the war.

Gossip flickers from sweating ghost to ghost –
Futures and unions, *gelt* grubbed and lost,
How the chains will force them all to the ditch,
Whose mother-in-law is the bigger bitch –
But sure as grain grinds down millstone grooves
Talk rumbles round to ancestral Jews,
English fades to Yiddish, newspapers fall,
Badinage ends, a defendant's called.

It could have been Toledo, without the Cross.

Trial begins in time-honored fashion,
Sheeted bencher posing Arendt's question:
How could you go like cattle to slaughter?
You don't understand, a big man mutters,
We thought we were going to labor camps.
Cheerful cards arrived with Polish stamps.
Selections done some went to the 'showers'
From the platform clutching soap and towels.

It could have been Łódź Ghetto, without dogs.

He crooks an arm above his head as though
Once more to block a kapo's blow,
Baring a hallmark as his sheet shakes loose,
Faded black numbers from a crude tattoo
Done on arrival, each jab in the arm
Rending the garment his tribe had worn
For ages, cut from study, ancient texts,
Phylacteries bowed above stiff necks.

Der malechamoves oyf a shvartze ferd.

Some turn away to rekindle a smoke,
Re-crossing a leg, or slurping a Coke
From half-full, dingy plastic cup; none eyes
That numbered forearm. Silent they lie,
Mulling the quiet registers of fear
Till stink of groin and armpit disappear,
Then reassure themselves by finding fault,
Saying these should have run, those should have fought.

It could have been Gehenna, babes and all.

Rosebud

Peace cut war's three shifts to one,
Folks sold up and streets turned slum
Where six days a week Dad kept store,
Each year worse than the one before.

He watched me eye an English bike,
Black steel bright in a shop at night,
When one went by, swivel and stare,
Heard me beg friends for rides on theirs
And my voice fall watching his fist
Wad register tapes at breakfast.

Happy birthday was all he said
Handing me that thoroughbred
I rode to school next day, locked
And at the final bell forgot,
So long a dream it slipped my mind
Till I walked back to school at nine
And saw it hanging, bent, flensed,
A skeleton on the school fence
That would not race again.
                                        Peccavi
And his poised strap haunted me
Home to supper, confession, bed
In tears.
                    Dawn: he shook me, eyes red,
Free from my twisted covers
To find a second virgin racer.

We never spoke about those Raleighs.
Perhaps my fallen face recalled the
Depression corner where he hawked apples
with his father, memory of an older brother
pedaling past to high school while he walked
to work, or something from his favourite film,
Citizen Kane. Now I cannot know. Old myself,
when I survey the wreck we make of life
he comes to mind and the vessel rights:
in balance with what's worst, two bikes.

Ishmael

And he will be a wild man;
his hand will be against every man
and every man's hand against him.

Genesis 16:12

1

My father fished three days a week,
A maid helped mother clean and mend,
My brother's hands stayed soft and weak
And I was sent to the cold with men.

Swaddled in white coat chin to uppers
I trained from twelve to butcher meat
And dress it on enamelled platters,
Fat tucked like toes under bound feet;
Played Philoctetes to fowl bones,
Saw blue line crawl my ulnar vein,
Hied septic blood to wards alone
For antidote to purge the stain;
Made green meat red with dye and grinding,
Saw cutting rooms break men by fifty;
Stood behind a dumpster pissing
To save time when we were busy.

No angels graced that wilderness,
No wells, no Hagar, no augur
Sifting offal who foretold success
Beyond cleaver and block; no wonder
Drug for a child's mind gone tough,
No acne salve to hide the blush
When the father of a puppy love
Sniffed at the sawdust in my cuff.

Roots cankered past disinfection
I gave my back to home and nation,
Alien with alien vision,
Cancers present, though in remission.

2

A rusted ring bolt and long length of chain
Lie on the asphalt where a black dog prowls;
The hairless weal around its neck makes plain,
As well as spade ears, fangs, gun barrel snout
That this mailed compound long has been home.
Gates bear no warning; there's no need to snarl;
Scarred skin, the rasp while gnawing at a bone
Guarantee junked cars in nearby piles
Rest undisturbed and rot alone.

IV

Accounting

You subtracted the *i* you added
to your name in junior high,
so spelling and how I said it
matched, from the note returning
my faded blue air letters, three
decades and a final, frank drink on,
purging my account of all but
spectres that absent vowel starts –

the dawn offer, *Say you love me*
and things will be different, breathed
in your family row house after
prom; counterfeiting payment
as I tore your teenage hymen;
our preemie bastard by-product
buried, unnamed, in hours;
exchanging vows to ease your loss
with fingers crossed behind my back;
the spouse swap I thought would leave me
quits, when his wife welshed but you
turned trick, your folded dainties
neatly spread on the chair beside
our bed and semen you called
sweat oozing from your housecoat's fly;
packing the car, throwing you out –

But closing books is hard to do
when one release requires two.
Now from orthography I see
you have done dickering with me
and I can set those ledgers by
in which I used to tick and tie,
labouring from false beginning
to strike a balance out of sinning.

Death Rattle

I came round to the juddering gasp and wheeze
Of an unconscious man wrestling air to breathe
Through phlegm his cortex could not instruct
His throat to clear, like the in-out suck
Of a red-faced asthmatic praying for
Ephedrine to work. I gave him no more
Thought, noted falling snow, wondered instead
Was my new car radio alive or dead,
But could not move my fingers to find out.

Blood vessels close; behind the id's redoubt
The moral mind curls like a porcupine
Balled against a dog, unaware of time,
Guarding itself against the casualty,
Mentor and friend, crumpled beside me.

Blind Date

And while we spoke of many things, fools and kings…
Nat King Cole, 'Nature Boy'

She stands apart,
Teal suitcase, heels, flesh pantyhose,
Belted black wool dress that rose
Knee-high when she stepped off the bus
Into the Friday evening's fuss
Of co-eds handing baggage down
To Yalies milling on the ground,
And scanned each kissing couple
For an outlier, a double,
Brows circumflex like hers to sign
The stranger both half fear to find.

He talks all night,
Through 'thirties ersatz gothic halls,
Past cloister, quad, library stalls,
Dinner in the refectory,
Dead tapes booming at a party,
In the law dorm room on loan
So she may go to sleep alone,
A white stick stumble through a dance
Learned as barter, not romance
From pre-Pill girlfriends who were paid
With promises in time gainsaid.

She sits at sunrise,
A Pre-Raphaelite, hem spread
Across bare feet on a single bed,
Immobile, silent, listening
To her distant date summoning
Ghosts, his back hard against the door,
Staring at spots on the oak floor,
Extends her hand, pats the cover
And whispers *Will you come over?*

Over, over, the buoys moan,
Fog-bound sailor, follow me home.

Texaco Saturday Afternoon Opera

But this or such was Bleistein's way
T.S. Eliot, 'Burbank with a Baedeker: Bleistein with a Cigar'

Talk sputters out, house lights lower,
A white wand rises with the scrim
And I see Chick not Lohengrin
White coat and apron amid clutter,
Salt beef, herrings, dills in brine,
Rye bread piles three feet high
Crusted with mountaineering flies,
Stone streets outside his deli lined
With trash, graffiti walls and doors
Where derelicts in newsprint quilts
Doze like rank question marks on silt,
Cadillacs, pimps, and fat-arsed whores:
Childhood holograms that contain
Lunchbreak sights when I worked with dad.

Two decades on, a Yale Law grad,
I have come back, first class, by plane
To survey all with widened eyes –
Dying neighbourhood, dying shop,
Anglicised surname a prop
Above steel grates – unrecognised
Until I interrupt the Jew
Making sandwiches. *Danila?*
I puff up to launch my vita…

A radio warns curtain's due,
His welcome turns apology:
It's starting now, I've got to go,
The Met's doing 'Seraglio'.

The store goes dark, the patron keys
The lock and leaves me curb-side, stunned,
Complacencies of the Courts undone
By an old shopkeeper's passion.

Cabaletta

'I remember every detail…'

Rick to Ilsa, *Casablanca*

Lunch *à deux* dwindles to shadows
In a glass-walled garden dining room
Where Bacons frame late afternoon
And the chatelaine's Sloane Square repose.
Exes exhumed cue memory,
Stylus settles in a worn track
A betrothed cut decades back
Who dropped him like a sherry
Glass chance knocks to a marble floor,
Scattering sparkling shard and mite
Some Athens maid may sweep from sight
But no craftsman can restore,
And resurrects the dress she wore,
Gray A-line, scarlet hem and cuff,
Collar fringed with white lace ruff,
Matching gray Alice band to snare
Her fall of shoulder-length red hair,
Sashaying down a dorm hall stair
At Vassar forty years before…

The hostess interrupts the score:
You think about her every day?
The question hangs, he looks away,
Ticks a tine whose chime recalls
Gold leaves at dusk, a last curt call,
The click of tumblers when they fall

And lifts the tone arm from the platter,
Pushes back a few breaths later,
Rises with *Sorry, thanks, a busy week,*
But will not press milady's cheek.

All The Dark Years

Casements open on lawns and river,
croquet, gowns, a tutor tamping his meerschaum,
the young man opposite talking Yeats...
swamp soapbox scooters skirling through
treeless streets; Uncle Abe, slacks grey
with Havana ash, meting punishment
in curses to dead-beat gamblers and
grafting cops; a legless vet shaking
pencils in a cap... I bob amongst a
golden cohort, where summer is a verb,
tea follows sport, after dinner *chocolate*
liqueurs and port; conjure a cave-fish
risen from Erebus, blind in the light.

Olympus dazzled me: *Esq.*
embossed on letterhead, black wool bespoke
suits from the Row, walnut wainscot meeting
rooms, white marble columned porticoes,
idling limousines, private jets, lunches
brokered for senators and CEOs
who dine to barter tax bills, cash and votes,
finning in stews worse than my spawning
ground, a fingerling in thrall to shadows.

All the dark years haunt me. Not what happened –
the follies, lust, greed and pride, paying out
their trawls behind me; the muggings,
knives poised behind the office arras,
a *Dear John* call from a WASP fiancée;
time in the stocks – but warnings missed
because I could not gauge what others felt,
whirling face down in eddies of the self.

For John Crook

(1921–2007)

Punts and crowds are gone from the Backs,
Christmas clears the Courts, only swans
And red-kneed choristers leave tracks
Where the winter of his words immures a Don
Indifferent to honours,
But not his College, or its scholars.

We he tutored, who would physic
What soon departs, discover
We're still charges; though a catheter
From gut to turn-up drains waste
He cannot pass, and a wheelchair
Rolls him past gardens he once paced,
He counters all concern the same,
I am decaying, croaked to bar
Us mounting his stairwell again
On concave steps to succour
A classicist dying in his rooms alone,
Slumped by a gas fire in an armchair,
Skin sloughed from mandible and thighs,
Reading Georgian poetry to bear
Decay's degenerate surprise.

We must prepare, nearing his set
For clarinet stilled, speech fled;
Prepare, should he grant a visit,
And feign not to notice what's unsaid.

Homage for a Waterman

He jams his clam tongs down three feet
and fetches bottom, pulls them so wide
he leans spread-eagled, then scissors
back, heaving till his knuckles meet,
and hoists the bales over the side
hoping for little necks or oysters,
a black oil-skinned stick figure
pile-driving in November sleet.

Townies charter him in season
to cast the bars with bright lead lures
or eels, a year's bookings complete
before it starts, and find him on
the dock at dawn, a white sweatshirt,
khakis, red and black plaid coat,
a Triton other skippers query
on where to run, what wrecks to skirt.

Thirty years ago time took his boat,
in due course him, then his parties;
where he rests, an urn, beneath a stone,
I never learned, while the boy
who begged to help his hero lift
the hook wears plastic knees for bone.
But when winds sough and sea gulls toy
with thermals by my hollowed cliff
his leathered face looms into sight
through spray and howl, helm held tight,
bow to seas breaking in the bight.

Facsimile Folio

A blank flyleaf augurs pristine leaves
In the Folio you gave me years ago
Exhumed today where it lay un-sleeved
Beneath my current lady's books and clothes.
My fingers trek from first page through to last
(Although I know nothing awaits me there)
Searching for a message that slipped past
Earlier explorations down the years,
The way a Qumran scholar's finger scrapes
Encrusted Aramaic scripts for clues
The saviour Jesus Christ to whom he prays
Was foretold by a splinter sect of Jews.
    That searched-for text I shall not find;
    The lines are writ only in my mind.

John Winthrop's Ghost

Waved over by that flaming brand: the gate
With dreadful faces thronged and fiery arms.

Paradise Lost, XII, ll. 43–4

We were baptized in a fable
Got by heart when we were able,
That peruked enlightened men
Wielding Locke and a quill pen,
Europe's peasants with raised eye
Watching *Liberty* slide by,
Ex-slaves hollering hosannas,
Heroes in the Marianas,
Built a city on a hill.
We believed, as children will,
Marched to Souza for assembly
Behind scouts trooping Old Glory
To stand in ranks, each kid a rod,
Pledging *One nation under God!*

A .38 swung from a nail below
The till in my father's butcher shop
Where I scrubbed platters when I was nine;
Rats scuttled behind the washing barrel.
Unscripted hours left for play, and vacant
Summers when a social self is schooled,
I waited trade and learned decimals
Padding bills by five percent, or cross
Hatched my hands with wire rope cuts
Working fishing boats off the Jersey shore.

Klondike dreams we mined from *Life*:
Lawns, tall man and leggy wife,
Sandy blonds in tennis white,
Kids captioned saying goodnight
At cocktail time, Brahmin names,
Eliot, Lowell, Cabot, James,
Grand Yankee university:
Base metals for Gatsby alchemy.

England refinished me, spun hempen
Into worsted from mill ends of ideas
And sherry teas in limestone Tudor courts,
Softened 'G's to cantillate the creed,
Then shipped me home to attend the ivy-
Towered masters of New England. Ticket
Punched, sporting a blue-eyed, Christian
'Cliffie, I pushed open Wall Street's doors
Where John Winthrop's ghost waylaid me
And slit my suit to prove my bones were sound.

Rigid old spook, I sucked your myths
Like mother's teats, re-cut my cloth
In great mills of the mind, donned
Correct commercial braces: why the question?
But nothing suited me for dinner
Tables in America; I had become
An alloy skittering across the land
Like sodium on water, a rasp
Annealed past transformation as a boy
In acids that eat the white off sepulchres,
Apostate to *Election*, *frum* in doubt,
Grit in an oyster duly spat out.

V

Pastiche

When we two parted
In – was it two years? –
I keen to be started,
You blinking back tears,

Agreed before wedding,
Sealed with a toke,
The vows we were swearing
Were sworn for your folk,

You honored our treaty,
divorced by consent,
Spared argy-bargy
And waved when I went.

Marriage was cover,
(That was our claim),
To spite your mother,
To bank an old flame;

You dated others,
Dwelled far apart,
And fifteen years later
Gave one man your heart.

Now well past sixty,
I've asked you to dine,
And flown to your city
An ocean from mine

To thank you for hiding
When we said goodbyes,
Doors you were closing,
Your darkening eyes.

Poetry Reading

You turn and face me now
All Bala-Cynwood in your Peter Pan
Collar, and single strand of pearls

L.E. Sissman, 'On the Island'

You turn and face me now
Five feet ten in running
Shoes on the balcony
Of my London hotel
Room, model's form unsexed
By baggy running dress,
Looking incongruous
Dear ageing Irish miss
Reading poems from my
Book, open at your waist.

Who would think it's what it
Is, sadly has ever
Been, equilibristic,
Not preface to darting
Tongues and sticky bliss,
Merely our unspoken
Excuse to lift the scrims
On other poems, read
To others, at other trysts.

After Lunch

Mach two the green sign glows;
You're far behind
Fifty thousand feet shows.
And far below.

Crew start dinner service,
We ate hours back,
Ask 'Scotch, soda, claret?'
Our voices low.

Gladly I'd have missed this plane,
Had you but asked,
To run with you again at dawn
Hyde Park's pale rose-lined paths.

Little Black Dress

My carriage straight, your bosom taut,
I courted you smartly, as young men ought,
Applauded your shape in a little black dress,
Followed your arms as they rose to undress.

Now frames are bent, our breastwork sags,
And the little black dress is gone for rags.
So I court you gently, as old men must,
With a shade less ardor, a bit less fuss.

Kept

We fly hand in hand DC to Boston
Above chartreuse shoots, animal riots,
Milter-crammed creeks, drunk on the season
And transgression. Before the hallway quiets
Behind the bellman, we lock and topple
To the sheets, dinner deferred. I wear no
Ring to scold us while we tumble.

Myrtle
Green leaves shade lunch, your skin's pregnant glow,
My averted eyes and nod to a rescission
Silence made you volunteer: we don't meet
Again.

Today I found your note, the one
About *...what's done for love...a quondam beat...*
Buried in bumf unearthed for cremation,
A mystery still, something I can name
But never trust, and keep it from the flame.

Pas de Deux

Cranach's Eve in black silk pants
Strokes his sleeve: 'Perhaps a dance?'
He takes her arm and tries the chance
With *entrechats* of compliments
To show he'll partner her intent –
'Black becomes you' then leaps again,
'I came for you' – while walking in
To dine at cocktail hour's end.

Adultery begins like this.

A *glissade* to James and Wharton,
Masters of repressed emotion
Suggests a theme beyond flirtation
And intellectual foreplay,
One he floats with a *grand jeté*
Confessing to his last affair,
A step he risks so that the pair
May talk of what has brought them there.

Adultery begins like this.

Knee pressed to knee, so close heads turn,
Their whispers damn what they might burn
At their age for a final passion,
Post-coital sweat, enervation's
Languorous kind conversations,
Wedding rings and guilt in balance
With one last abandoned prance
To charge senescence with romance.

Adultery begins like this.

Coffee, port and Sauternes done
All rise, the soiree's coda come,
Thank the hosts, air-kiss and run.
He proffers cheek, like any friend,
Unsure how their ballet should end.
'Oh, must I always lead?' she sighs
En pointe, spread hand lifted to hide
His mouth while her tongue slips inside.

Adultery began like this.

Winter Mornings

Through frost I navigate Hyde Park
As shapes loom from ebbing dark
When one, red hair drawn back and tied
Above high cheekbones, piques my eyes
Which slit to focus. I crane, slack
Way, as last resort change tack
To scout the prize I seem to see.

The western sea splits you from me,
As do your children, husband, faith,
You lie past reach of sail, a wraith.
I know the odds. But still I stare
At a thin stranger walking there,
Like a dawn watch too long at sea
Hailing landfalls that cannot be.

Yester-year

A decade on fog conjures you,
Although we have not met again.
I moor with wraiths at sixty-two.

There was no plan to lie, untrue,
My scruples strangled in your mane
(A decade on, fog conjures you)

When I dismissed what looks might do,
By northern seas at summer's wane.
I moor with wraiths at sixty-two.

Your spouse, my best friend, never knew
You shipped him off to stain his name.
(A decade on fog conjures you.)

How we veered, no longer two,
Toward wreck of marriages and fame,
(I moor with wraiths at sixty-two)

Till shame stilled the gale that blew
Left me a hulk, sheets foul, struck main.
A decade on fog conjures you.
I moor with wraiths at sixty-two.

Revenant

For her I did what I had done with others,
Unpicked the cloth woven over years
From wealth, art and anger into armour
That fit like skin after wear and tears
To show how scorn and grief had fashioned
Armatures to build my masks upon.
What if this autopsy for an old passion
Disturbed a ghost or raised a storm?

But she shook me with her capers in the snow,
Her child's smile waking to see the dawn
And I was silent when she rose to go,
An iconoclast receding down my lawn
While I toed shattered fictions at my feet
Watching dust trail her departure through the trees.

Sie Kommt

(…Es ist die Königin der Nacht…)

Tamino in *The Magic Flute*

She comes with a train of shadows never cast
By any earthly forms whose charge and mass
Thwart light; they flutter just beyond my grasp
Like cherry blossoms a puff of wind unclasps.

She comes around the corner of the years
Streaming faux memories from foreign piers
That never were, dreams I would clear
Of unshared passages, landfalls and tears.

She comes and, for a breath, regret unveils
An unmade voyage: our first-born's squall,
Trimming the sheets while teaching her to sail,
Her hand on mine before my father's pall.

Phantoms swimming in my deeps of night,
No magic flute can pipe you to the light.

The Faithful

Will you reconnoitre after lunch,
Alone, mobile in hand for an urban
Nook from which to call where you
Will not be seen or heard, masking
Your aim like a jihadi, pleading
Exercise rather than 'Asr prayers?
If so, when you find a spot and press
The green key will blue paper catch
Sparking a blast across the sea?

Muslim martyrs are no different,
Dear, from you and me; sweet success
Will shatter both our worlds,
Though we may be more certain
Than they what our deserts will be.

End of the Affair

It ends soundlessly: my hand slips yours
To adjust demeanour for a neighbour,
No bang, bombed body sprawled, no prayer,
Just a gentle unlacing of fingers
Wrests warp from woof in the tapestry we
Fashioned from Fragonards and poetry
To decorate our idyll. We stand
Naked by the roadside with vagrant hands,
Sunlit in senescent imperfection,
My stoop and vanished waist, runt canyons
Time and disappointment wore in your face,
In silence that surrounds a fall from grace
And separate soon after, sans goodbye,
Relieved what never lived had died.

VI

Decorating the Nursery

Was I surprised after a year's dispatches
About uxorial combat and its consequences,
Court convoyed visits to your daughter,
Old friendships sunk, financial slaughter,
The different mayhem each day brings,
When suddenly unbowed, gamboling
You came a-maying with a new consort
Half-Venus, half-Penelope by your report
Who is already 'decorating the nursery'
While your hearth seethes with hostilities?
Not really: consider Chinook, perhaps,
Leaping water ladders with a tail slap,
Scales shimmering rainbow in anticipation,
Rushing to their deadly assignation.

Wine Circle

Black gowns flap from dinner's tart and cream
To port in Senior Common Room upstairs,
Sit round the Master in the coal fire's gleam
And preen the intellects that brought them there.
They wheel aloft, circling schools of thought,
Above superstition and sentiment,
Dive on weak theses in maths or art, squawk
As they dismember faulty arguments.
But like us all, falcons wear hoods and wait,
One wants his ashes after death to sit
Potted by the Fellows near the fire grate,
Another came to Christ in a Gobi pit.
The tapers gutter, old birds collapse,
Spilt wine mingles with melting candle wax.

Dodge-Ball

Standing behind a lectern on a box
To see above the microphones cocked
To catch my words, cornered in a pen
Made of clicking shutters and shouting men
I lost my way, Cortez above the sea.
No slave whispered 'memento mori',
I never saw jackals in the shadows
Holding their pens like Herculean arrows
In wait for cripples from dodge-ball games,
Or the bullet coming, like Jesse James.

In the Empty Quarter no phones ring
Lunch goes undone, the caravan dwindles.
You sit alone sorting hate mail and bills
For futures bought on notoriety,
Fingering mistakes and credulities
Like a mumbling Bedouin's palsied hand
Telling prayer beads in a parched land.

When the dogs and kites rose from their mess
I downed Ecclesiastes, stiffed the press,
Stuck poultices to flesh where skin had been,
Traded leathers for suits, tucked a foulard in
And walked once more over London Bridge
Into the City.
     Defeat is a scourge
That changes men: I'm always wary now,
Flinch from compliments, pat each smile down
For the powdered purpose that harbours grief
And welcome old age as a blessed thief
Who will steal me to the dark beyond the reach
Of light to read and this damned rage for speech.

Blue Rinse Matrons

A blue rinse matron and her blue rinse friend
Waft down a Maine coast village street.
Her cook heaves into view at the far end
On a course that will see these vessels meet.
Crows' nests register the closing ground,
The lesser craft readies a proper greeting,
But the capital ships wear slowly round
And give their sterns to the tender passing.
Their maneuver's not extraordinary,
Logs are full of similar altered courses
To avoid a beggar, mumbling loony
Or ruined friend who once shook bourses:
    Recall the *St. Louis* un-disembarked
    Standing east from Havana into the dark.

Momentum

Lumps she felt probing her chest
A surgeon cut out with her breast,
Then chemo, x-rays, hairy combs,
Time congealed in waiting rooms
Where strangers wonder if they'll live
Clutching lover or relative,
Rogue cells that for a time refrain
From their blitzkrieg in her brain,
Prostheses, wigs and summer airs
Demote the enemy to scares;
And when she hears *There's no hope left*,
Life still negotiates with death.

Yards pull the boats, staff cover chairs,
The Season dwindles into air;
Her body gives disease its head:
Skin slackens, viper toxins spread,
A morphine drip stands by the bed,
Veins, vocal cords and bowels block,
The long coats check in round the clock
Until, fly-wheel whirled to rest
She rots to repast for a pest.

Man imitates cosmology,
From grinding groins to elegy,
Primeval bang to nothingness,
From emptiness to emptiness,
Bone, nerve and muscle cling to breath:
In the death camps, few chose death.

Three Sonnets on the Coup de Grâce

1

She stands by the bed, breath caught, murderess
To be, no Borgia, but a county belle
Gone fifty, in a red rumpled dress
Witness to her night watch for a senile
Man reeking of rubbing liniment
For bed sores (*Is this still my father?*),
Moaning, insensible, incontinent
(*Is this husk him?*).
      Her hands spasm, hover
Near drip and catheter doctors won't forego,
Grab, then tape a pillow to white stubble;
The body writhes below, life won't let go.
The saviour drops her weapon and scuttles
Off in tears.
     Drunk, at times she'll corner
A stranger and confess her distaff failure.

2

A black aide bends to an ancient lady
And says, *Honey, your son's come*, cranks up her
Bed, adjusts oxygen to oil creaky
Breathing, then dips once more, announcing *Dear,
He's here*. Thin lids flicker, she croaks until
She says his name, is stuporous again.

We wait for death to wring pulse from her shell,
But that's harder now, overdose risks blame,
Perhaps indictment, and so her dark angel
Changes rôles to charm life from its host. She coos
Le'go darlin', it's OK to go, to gentle
Breath away and cut the carcass loose,
A soft command to help her charge depart,
Words whispered hemlock to halt a heart.

3

He came to in Recovery, the cancer
in his bowels past knife or chemistry
to cure, the 'D.N.R.' he'd asked for
on the chart the intern read, and put to sea
a last time, alone.
               They took my captain's
license last year; I'm on my third pacemaker:
when it comes, just leave and close the curtains…
(his hand curls), *remember, my kids are lawyers.*

His aorta burst two hours later
and we draped all the mirrors that night.
There was no will, he had no plate, or
bonds, or land, what men leave that they might
dam the river Lethe. Still, we felt blest,
he left us as he lived for his bequest.

Uphill to the Right

Uphill to the right
You'll find
The house I built
In my prime
With cedar shingles
And tall glass to watch
The North Atlantic
Gnaw these rocks,
And in the courtyard
On a bench inscribed
Four words,
Man is a passerby.

Manqué

Through fog blown inland off the sea
By tumbled walls amidst old trees
Summoning verse from memory
That others wrote, I walk my land,
A stiff-kneed quondam businessman
Fixed on Ulysses, lesser men,
Faded notes, a dry pen,
And fear, push come to shove,
I am no good at what I love.

VII

Compounds

1

Gone the asphalt soldier
From sand, steppe and polder,
The camps razed or left
Consecrated to death,
The culture shattered,
Its thinkers scattered,
And banners turned smoke
In stoves warming the Volk.

2

The feral enterprise put down
What remains of it are nouns
Strewn across the fields of thought
Like salt over a barren plot;
Vanilla words for gruesome aims
Like *Endlösung* and *Judenrein* –
'Final Solution', 'clean of Jews' –
Einsatzgruppen for killing crews.

3

The sovereignty of words declines
Through ignorance, distortion, time
Or when misery they describe
Befalls some other distant tribe:
A pot scorching an infant's hand
Teaches a lesson to the man
His son in turn will have to learn
At a like age, with a like burn.

4

Tunis rises where Rome sowed
Al Aqsa rests on Temple bones
At Passchendaele the cattle low
In Nagasaki gardens grow:
Ash blackens, rain clears the skies,
Pain ends when the creature dies.

Modern Painters

He trowels whites and pewters, builds a base,
Carves his oils, smears, brushes, pastes.
Black strokes for bones incise a skinless face
On an ochre field. Canvas erased,
Heaped with paint again, again effaced,
Bequeaths a palimpsest of skin and grace,
Until at last the human mask's replaced
With slabs of flesh like a filleted fish.

We look like this after things fall apart;
The painting is the autopsy report
From an inquest where war took the part
Of coroner. The scalpel lifts to start:
Invade, split ribcage, scour thought and art,
Slit pericardium, inspect the heart;
Grab forceps, rip the viscera apart,
That heap of faiths and old philosophies

Covering the mean midden of descent,
And expose in the entrails of events
A rail-head, barbed wire ligaments,
Wounds savage beyond both Testaments'
Prophecies. With this dismemberment
The curtain fell on the Enlightenment,
Like *Luftmenschen* ash blacking Red regiments
On their slow slog west from Stalingrad.

A Brewing Tale

And from thenceforth Pilate sought to release him: but the Jews cried out...
Away with Him, away with Him, crucify Him.

St. John 19:12–15

Saint John distilled bitter brews
Ages ago for kindred Jews
Who pooh-poohed his Master's dictum
Life gets better after this one.
Taste for his Gospel-potion spread
From holy land to Holyhead
Slaking a thirst for rationale
To pen *Ostjuden* in the Pale,
Deny them land and make them grovel,
Apostatise and torch their hovel,
Then the final retribution:
Industrial mass execution.

From such ancient, toxic ichors
Who would dream of blending liquors?
And yet, despite aeons of fencing
To baulk Hebe and Goy from yentzing,
Slap their young malts side by side,
Add time, and they debouch a tide
Swollen with *mischlings* when in spate
That bursts the hoops of church and state,
Fermented by a Lord who dwells
Where civet cannot mask the smells.

The Lesson

there is not a man in the earth
to come in unto us after the manner of
all the earth

Genesis 19:31

A brimstone stench rises from rotting dead,
Shrouding the salted mother where she stands
On high ground, facing homeward till she melts,
While in a cave her virgin girls assay
The moral smoldering at their backs, and scheme:
Come, let us make our father drink and we
Will lie with him and so preserve his seed.

Raw-eyed, noses stuffed with sodomites'
And blasphemers' ash, they honor a power
Greater than all there are, and ever were.
Each daughter rapes, each one conceives a child:
The Jordan does not run red, no locusts come,
Their incestuous bellies swell uncondemned.

When seedling cypress crack the lava lid
Tamping bones from Sodom and Gomorrah's dead
Lot's daughters squat on birthing pans
Expelling brothers into their father's hands.

Rigoletto

First Aria

This or that one, it's all the same
To me: if they cling, I flick them
Off like fleas; nothing – menses, name,
A lady's plea – halts the game
Until I come.

No one hisses when he strides on stage.
Young tenors queue to play the part.
Neither censors nor the godly rage
When murmuring crowds depart
Humming his tunes.

Last Aria

Gilda lies sacked at her father's feet
while the man she died for sings offstage:

Woman is mutable,
Fluttering gossamer,
Born undependable,
Bred for a liar;
Yet we will deify
Proud teats, a bent bow seat
Loathe but must lie
With her, like we must eat.

The hunchback keens, lights dim, we hush.
The libertine strolls off unscathed.

Curtain Call

Confess, we come for the satyr,
To revel in his bookend airs,
The perp, yet the one chance spares,
Stand for him at the finish, cheer
And clap the reprehensible;
High Cs alone, the victim's part
Don't rock substratum of a heart
The way that chthonic rogues will, thrill,
Rumble endorphins and release
Primeval musky reveries.

Summa

Ethics distils
To three *wills*:
　If I do it will I go to jail?
　　If I do it will I get paid?
　　　Will my wife find out if I get laid?
　　　The rest is embroidery.

Motes

Suppose it true Dr. Witten's strings
with ten-dimensional flutterings
spawn numberless realities,
would that make rock cloud, or pairs threes,
us strip less feverishly
after months apart, *Air on a G
String* jar, waves roll east beyond eyes' reach,
Against the wind, off a western beach?

I'd still peek over your belly
to watch you bite your arm in frenzy,
wear out CDs playing an English Suite,
laze in the surf cooling sand-burnt feet

and yet, our blue pebble would seem smaller,
like a child's room now the child's older.

Un Coup de Dés

Chance authors all we do,
The plot's contrived in retrospect.
Spied once I still look out for you;
Chance authors all we do.
A sea bird shot, a woman met
Un-gloving who then strolls from view
Alters to fate as we reflect.
Chance authors all we do,
The plot's contrived in retrospect.

Identity

Come: do not touch me: let me alone discover
The holy and funereal ground where I
Must take this fated earth to be my shroud.

Oedipus at Colonus
Grene and Lattimore, ll. 1544–46

Ego teeters on the tip of years
Honks a last horn, taps flippers, rears
To cheers and fish and waddles off,
An old thespian with a cough
Retreating to a circus cage
After a lifetime centre stage
To rot behind steel bars and wait.

Self examines the heap of time,
Hefts what's left, sifts what's behind,
Takes toddler tears, abiding pain
From rejection, not risked again,
Compacts the lot to stucco paste,
Concocts history from this waste
And plays Macaulay with your life.

I bursts the bonds of blood and bone
More often now as head grows bare –
Diving at dusk from a Greek cliff,
Heels rising over sea; sheets mussed,
Languorous beside a lover
For the first time; the House hushed
By a violin heralding
Violetta's death – being blanks,
Ego and *self* wink out, no sound, no
Clock ticks, no up, down, for a breath
All comes to view, maths' phantom strings
Shivering beneath the stars beside
A loathed or longed-for face,
Silver for sere indignities.

Beside a Cove

Beside a cove on the Gulf of Maine
Below a sheer pink granite mountain
Tourists stop where the road flattens
And gaze with natural piety,
No sighs, no trembling
For nature as a darkening thing.

And though not reverent, I too
Sometimes halt and stare at that view
Until mountain seems air not rock
And sea time, setting all to be
With all I see toward nullity,
No light, no land, oceans become
Stray particles near a dead sun,
Then with a nod walk on.

The Institute

A sign and ten low buildings pass
unnoticed in a field the size of Central
Park: a wallflower by a college town.
Wandering its halls, one-chair offices,
bare eggwhite walls, nothing stands out until
I reach a lounge where mathematical
notations – integers, fractions, powers,
roots, Greek letters, brackets, slashes – weave
arabesques of genesis and infant stars
for paper napkin audience and nibbled
chocolate bars, on slate where palimpsests
and marginalia in coloured chalks suggest
a coffee break authored this text
a plaque below it warns, DO NOT ERASE.

Today's news is no better than yesterday's:
three suicide bombings in the 'cradle
of civilization'; a dowager billionaire
in Voltaire's homeland gives her daughter's
patrimony to a decorator; tar balls seed
hot beaches in a spoiled land whose citizenry
always blame others; immortality remains
elusive and, *sub specie aeternitatis*,
there will be nothing. The same is forecast
for tomorrow, the one bright patch a blackboard
crammed with symbols I cannot understand,
guarded by three words, DO NOT ERASE.

Trade

Barnegat inlet is a gauntlet
In the sea, where waves break on sand
Bars that pen a bay, an unquiet
Place, lethal when easterlies stand
The long swells up to lumber
White-capped across the shoals
And crumble in a khaki welter
Of seaweed, mud and spray that rolls
West through the cleft Atlantic coast.

Charter-men say little on the docks
At dawn standing by for parties,
For mates to ready boats – pull chocks,
Dog ports and stow necessities,
Bait, ice and beer – for copper gleam
To port ahead, gulls working gore
From sand eel shoals the stripers glean,
Or terns on blue fins hours offshore,
The world shrunk to a compass rose.

After noon the wind comes up, skippers
Go topside, shout *Reel in!* and head
For home; crews gut the catch, scuppers
Clog with viscera, decks turn red
Till seawater sluices them teak
Again and sunburned weekend
Warriors, beers wedged, peaked,
Doze and in daydreams pretend
They're heroes home from the sea.

Lines secured, the anglers leave
For row homes, showers, bowling club:
But by slips boatmen remain, reeve
Rod guides, observe the weather, rub
Penetrant on rusted pliers
And pause – to watch sedge sway on flats,
Geese rise honking from wetland choirs,
The sun decline, a whirl of gnats
And the Light flick on at Barnegat.

Notes

'Death Mask'

S. Forbes, *A Natural History of Families* (Princeton, 2005), 'concisely examines what behavioural ecologists have discovered about family dynamics... [and] describes an uneasy union among family members in which rivalry for resources often has dramatic and even fatal consequences' (from the cover blurb to Forbes' book).

'The Apothetae', the place of throwaways, was a chasm at the foot of Mount Taygetus into which were thrown sickly Spartan infants.

'Inquisition'

'*schvitz*', '*platza*': see section II, pp. 45–47.

'*gelt*': Yiddish for 'money'.

'It could have been Toledo': the Inquisition Tribunal was established in Toledo in 1485. Twenty-five *autos-da-fé* were held in Toledo between 1485 and 1492, and 467 *conversos* were burned alive at the stake.

'It could have been Łódź Ghetto': the Łódź Ghetto was one of the largest in the *Generalgouvernement*, producing manufactures for the German war effort. All of its inhabitants were transported over two years to the death camp at Chełmno and gassed, the last of them in June 1944. The transportees were told they were being sent to munitions factories in Germany.
   Day-to-day affairs in the Łódź Ghetto were run by a *Judenrat*, or Jewish Council, whose president was the notorious Chaim Rumkowski, 'King of the Jews', who went to his death still protesting that by cooperating with the Germans at least some would be saved. His Jewish police were known for their ferocity in forcing Jews to obey their captors.

'*Der malechamoves oyf a schvartze ferd*' is Yiddish for 'the angel of death on a black horse' and suggests the idol Moloch, to whom babies were sacrificed at Gehenna by the Canaanites and, some scholars believe, the early Hebrews.

'Pas de Deux'

'Cranach': Lucas Cranach the Elder (1472–1553), a German painter at the court of the Elector of Saxony and close friend of Luther, painted several versions of the Fall, including *Adam and Eve* (1528), now in the Uffizi Gallery, Florence.

'Blue Rinse Matrons'

'Recall the *St. Louis* un-disembarked': the SS *St. Louis* left Hamburg on 13 May 1939 carrying a thousand Jews fleeing Germany. Cuba and the US refused to permit its passengers to disembark, and on June 7th the ship turned back to Europe, where many of its passengers were eventually murdered.